# THE KEY TO
# YOUR NEW HOME

# THE KEY TO YOUR NEW HOME

## A Primer of Liveable and Practical Houses

Edited by
### LEWIS STORRS, Jr.

**Whittlesey House**
**McGRAW-HILL BOOK COMPANY, INC.**
New York                                    London

4

PUBLISHED BY WHITTLESEY HOUSE
A division of the McGraw-Hill Book Company, Inc.
COPYRIGHT 1938 BY LEWIS STORRS, JR.
ALL RIGHTS RESERVED. MADE IN THE U. S. A.
BY THE TELEGRAPH PRESS, HARRISBURG, PA.

# CONTENTS

---

**6**

HARWELL HAMILTON HARRIS, DESIGNER

# PREFACE

The termination of the Second World War has opened the doors to the prospects of a period of peace and prosperity. Building a home of our own again becomes a reality.

During these past few years of denial, the postwar house of our dreams may have developed into some sort of magical dwelling, replete with all the latest in materials and mechanical equipment. It would be fine if we could select from among these many items, but undoubtedly some will never develop beyond the seductive magazine articles, and others will not be available for several years to come. While these improvements are tempting to think about, most of them are the ornaments of a building and will have little bearing upon whether a house is fundamentally successful or not.

At the same time, we have been making a steady and valuable progress with our thoughts relating to the design of a house. We are becoming eager to incorporate into the plan the ideas that will make our home an easier, brighter, and more economical place to sleep, eat, and play in. Awkward and superficial copies of historical styles of architecture have proved themselves unsatisfactory.

A liveable atmosphere and a practical plan are the most important assets a home can possess. A sheltered entrance is of more intrinsic value than a stylized façade that fails to protect the person arriving in the rain; a simple living room, planned around individual pieces of furniture, is more satisfactory than an elaborate one that does not adapt itself to congenial groupings; and a small bedroom with ample wall space for twin beds and easy access to a well-fitted dressing room is preferable to a much larger room with badly located doors and windows.

It is the thesis of this book that the successful home is created by making careful provision, first of all, for the small points that cater to the needs and pleasures of the owner. Next, the items that develop the individuality of the site, such as a large window to frame a pleasant view, must be taken into account. Then all of these factors must be coordinated into a practical and unified building that will be a thing of beauty and worthy of the name of architecture and not an uneconomical and disjointed assemblage of parts. This final integrating is a delicate task that requires the skill and artistry of the architect.

Such a method of procedure is the reverse of the more customary classical formula, which tries to fit the necessary accouterments of contemporary domestic life into a preconceived geometrical form. With this detailed approach to the problem, the plan develops from the inside out; it is organic and not mathematical. The house gains character when it expresses the personality of its owner.

When this attitude toward designing is taken, the drawbacks in imitating previous styles of architecture can be readily realized. Not only does copying put a damper on any progress toward the development of a better home, but the copy itself becomes more costly, and, at the same time, less satisfying than if an honest approach to the problem had been made. The Cape Cod cottage and the two-story colonial dwelling were excellent solutions for the living conditions of their day, but the world has changed a great deal since then.

The physical changes are too obvious to require more than mention. The automobile, electricity, plumbing, central heating, and new materials are among the more important developments which we can enjoy, and which must affect the planning of our houses.

Equally significant is the position of the home in modern life. It has lost a great deal of the importance it once had as the center of family life. Today, because of the automobile and the servant problem, a large part of one's life is spent outside of it. The home is no longer treated as an object to display before the public or as a symbol of a position to be maintained in the social structure. A sensible plan comes first. Each room has a function to perform and is not a mere ornament.

This book attempts to serve as a primer of the many details that can make a house both liveable and practical. It includes amenities as well as necessities. Some of the ideas presented will seem novel, while others will be familiar. However, it has been the aim to have each picture illustrate some definite point as well as be an attractive treatment in itself. Behind this has been the desire to express as far as is possible the crispness and freshness which result when a broad handling is permitted and which are essential in order to obtain the fullest enjoyment from a home.

H. ROY KELLEY, ARCHITECT

MARSTON & MAYBURY, ARCHITECTS

# THE EXTERIOR

GARDNER A. DAILEY, ARCHITECT

The design of the exterior of a house may be considered from several points of view. The facade may be treated as a romantic subject, a stage-set that attempts to recapture the glory of an Italian palace, of a Tudor manor house, of a Guilford "salt-box," or of some other historical model.

From another standpoint the thought may be to mould the building into a simple mass with a center entrance flanked by a balanced arrangement of wings and windows.

Again, the elevations may be developed frankly to represent the plan, with little if any striving for symmetry. Windows and doors are placed where they are most useful, but withal there is often a conscious effort to express the rooms within.

Still another philosophy regards the walls and roof as no more than a covering that encloses space and keeps out the weather, as though a sheet were spread over a rigid frame. Wall surfaces and openings are treated as areas to be patterned at will. The utmost freedom of design is thus granted. This fourth approach to the problem is still embryonic; it is evolving by means of the thoughtful application of new materials and methods of construction. Whatever may be the point of view, however, the finished building must have an emotional content; it must be a joy and not a mere utility.

Because of the physical and sociological changes that are occurring to-day, the home-builder is being more and more compelled to judge architectural features primarily by their practical value. This explains why in this book such emphasis has been placed on the details that compose the exterior instead of on complete facades. Even in the examples that show how a restful character may be imparted to a whole house, the expedients employed have been generally determined by a consideration of usefulness, and are not a superficial addition of lines. So that such features can be included in the design, an exterior treatment offering wide latitude is preferable to one that is limited by convention.

10

DOUGLAS HONNOLD, ARCHITECT

The two-story house on a narrow lot is apt to appear like a box, and look commonplace. It may be developed into a harmonious design by employing only a few elements, so that the facade is not cluttered with detail. A bold handling of these will lend distinction.

DONALD BEACH KIRBY, ARCHITECT

The proportions of a two-story house may be improved and a charm imparted by lowering the eaves from the normal position at the second-floor ceiling. This is done at the sacrifice of full ceiling height for the bedrooms. The cubage will figure less this way, but the actual cost will probably be more because of the extra work required for building dormer windows.

Long, horizontal lines on a facade give the optical illusion of a broader, lower building. The open pattern of the ironwork does not darken the windows below, but the solid center section of the hood shelters the doorway.

The front veranda, so popular at the turn of the century, is now too noisy and dirty for outdoor living in the city. Still, it supplies the best protection for the entrance and may be connected with a porte-cochere. The horizontal lines of the veranda cornice reduce the apparent height of the facade.

YOCH AND COUNCIL, LANDSCAPE ARCHITECTS

HONNOLD AND RUSSELL, ARCHITECTS

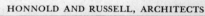

R. M. SCHINDLER, ARCHITECT

In this example the horizontal line is frankly designed as a unifying and restful feature, and yet is adapted to the needs of the house. It projects to shield the large glass areas on the right from excessive sunlight, then carries across the entrance porch to make a deeper recess, but becomes a part of the wall surface where the smaller windows do not require shading.

The second-story overhang, reminiscent of Seventeenth Century houses of New England, is another means of controlling the proportions of an elevation. In keeping with the house, the old-fashioned shed serves as prototype for the garage. This is easy to use, economical to build, and will protect the car in most weather. Doors may be added for severe climates.

GORDON B. KAUFMANN. ARCHITECT

ROLAND E. COATE, ARCHITECT

The strongest horizontal line is created by the covered balcony extending the full width of the facade, typical of the old buildings at Monterey. The overhang is enough to protect a walk to a drive. In warm weather the balcony can serve as communication between rooms. This treatment shades too many windows, however, so its use is limited.

The long, open balcony offers two advantages to this house. A strong horizontal line is effected, and the entrance is sheltered. At the same time, it does not cast a shadow on the windows below, for they are bayed out. See how the doorway depends upon form rather than detail for its effect.

WILLIAM WILSON WURSTER, ARCHITECT

PAUL R. WILLIAMS, ARCHITECT

A facade may still appear symmetrical even though a detail is not exactly balanced. This requires skill, but often imparts warmth and character to the building. The bay windows in this view are of the same size, but one has only a gentle curve while the other has a pronounced projection as well. The deep shadows of the porches with the brightness of the walls create an interesting pattern.

The two-storied portico offers protection from the weather without darkening the first-floor rooms. It will make a building impressive, but must be used cautiously, or it will efface the body of the house. The detailing of these columns shows how dignity and style are attained today with traditional forms, but without the ornateness of the recent Twenties.

ROLAND E. COATE, ARCHITECT, A. E. HANSEN, LANDSCAPE ARCHITECT

VAN PELT AND LIND, ARCHITECTS

The one-story house is particularly suitable where the lot is ample. The low, extended roof-lines avoid the stilted feeling that the two-story house sometimes gives. Notice how advantage has been taken of the tree in planning the drive; it acts as the center of the turn-around.

A semi-circular drive with a gentle curve leading to both garage and entrance is very easy to use. With such an arrangement backing is necessary only when leaving the garage. The double width required here by the two-car garage allows cars to be parked at the entrance without blocking the drive.

CURTIS CHAMBERS, ARCHITECT

SPENCER AND LANDON, ARCHITECTS

To include both a two-car garage and a house of any size on a lot as small as this one would have been impossible without putting one over the other. The stairway and balcony draw your attention away from the garage doors to the living quarters above. Notice how the plan conforms to the irregular shape of the lot.

The second story of a garage or outbuilding is adaptable to an office, studio or a suite of guest rooms, provided the approach is attractive and convenient. An exterior stair allows one to avoid the mess and grease of the ground floor, and can be interesting in itself.

GORDON B. KAUFMANN, ARCHITECT

15

PAUL R. WILLIAMS, ARCHITECT

Pavilions on large estates show a breadth of treatment and finish too often lacking in the small house. Behind the walls of one imagine a plan of your own. There may not be space for many bedrooms, but the effect is gracious nevertheless.

This is the other side of the pavilion above. The broad opening with sliding doors giving out upon the balcony and stairs is an idea that may be used to gain access to a lower garden from the living room of a hillside house, or to supply a direct approach to the ground from the bedroom of a two-story building.

PAUL R. WILLIAMS, ARCHITECT

HONNOLD AND RUSSELL, ARCHITECT

This pavilion might be helpful to the person who cherishes elegance, but has little money with which to attain it. A spacious living-dining room would fill the main mass in adapting it for living purposes. In the wing a bedroom or two with bath and a small kitchen could be included.

If you want large areas of glass, but are afraid of the glare, especially with a southern exposure, build a hood over the opening. Here the glass is divided into two sashes, which slide back, converting the enclosed lounge into an open porch. A swimming pool will be built on this side, complementing the tennis court on the other.

ROLAND E. COATE, ARCHITECT
YOCH AND COUNCIL, LANDSCAPE ARCHITECTS

H. ROY KELLEY, ARCHITECT
KATHERINE BASHFORD, LANDSCAPE ARCHITECT

The restraint and good taste of this pavilion are all the more appreciated when one realizes how easy it is to be tempted by the picturesque for a building of informal character in such a woodland setting. The wing on the lower level contains the dressing rooms; the main house is further down

For some people the pleasure of owning a place in the country depends primarily on developing it into a miniature farm. Barnyards, fences, dovecotes, gazebos and weathervanes may be added from time to time. With plenty of land for a setting they do not conflict with the design of the house as they would on a small city lot.

GORDON B. KAUFMANN, ARCHITECT

MARSTON AND MAYBURY, ARCHITECTS

Farm buildings offer the simplest means of enclosing space to keep out the weather. They depend primarily on mass and color for their effect. From them can be gained a pointer or two for the home that must have size at the expense of detail. This example shows the inherent beauty possible to this type of building.

Other things being equal, you can count upon a building of simple mass, honestly conceived, to be more satisfying than one cut up and into, and which draws forth the cry of "Cute!" at first sight. The low-pitched gable roof without dormers or intersecting wings is restful, and naturally the most economical to construct.

HETH WHARTON, ARCHITECT

THOMAS D. CHURCH, LANDSCAPE ARCHITECT

The approach from a crowded highway to an open motor court and then into the hall may be made more gradual by the inclusion of a walled entrance court. Slowly the character of the house is allowed to unfold, like the prelude to an opera. The parterre of boxwood is effective against the extreme simplicity of the architecture.

In the latter part of the Nineteenth Century double entrance doors were in high favor, but they have suffered in the reaction against things Victorian. They seem more hospitable and elegant than the single door, possibly on account of their proportions.

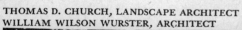

THOMAS D. CHURCH, LANDSCAPE ARCHITECT
WILLIAM WILSON WURSTER, ARCHITECT

CHARLES O. MATCHAM, ARCHITECT

For the one-story house an inexpensive way to shelter a walk to a drive is to extend the roof three feet or so beyond the face of the wall. This house also shows how materials themselves may play a part in the design. The entrance is emphasized by the contrast of its smooth wood finish with the coarse stone tile wall.

This entrance is definitely a contemporary solution, and yet the delicate round windows and the clever planting have an Oriental air. When seeking such effects, how much better to proceed as here, and be certain first that the demands at present-day living will be satisfied!

EDGAR BISSANTZ, ARCHITECT

ROLAND E. COATE, ARCHITECT

For bringing the planting right to the entrance an object resembling an oversized window-box may be used. It is of particular value where there is a paved terrace, for the blooms will add a cheerful note in season. The rest of the time evergreens or ivy can be used.

WINCHTON LEAMON RISLEY, ARCHITECT

To brighten the hall, an entrance door may be flanked by areas of glass ("side lights"), and have a transom at the top. Thus a broad and welcoming entrance motif is provided. Knobs look well on a pair of doors when centered as done here.

A covered passage to the drive not only marks the entrance to the house, but is truly appreciated in stormy weather when using the automobile. It may be treated in the simplest fashion with square, wooden posts and exposed rafters, as here.

The transition between drive and entrance may be effected by an open terrace. Shelter is not provided from the weather, but the paved area prevents an automobile from approaching close enough to the doorway to block the entrance. Notice how the planting boxes are incorporated into the design of the porch.

ROLAND E. COATE, ARCHITECT
KATHERINE BASHFORD, LANDSCAPE ARCHITECT

KEMPER NOMLAND, ARCHITECT

PAUL R. WILLIAMS, ARCHITECT

Instead of treating the electric fixture at the entrance as a necessary evil, it may be made the focal point of the whole design, and placed in a position that will provide adequate illumination for both door and steps. Too often the danger of darkened steps is forgotten, and the hospitality suggested by a bright doorway ignored.

The small entrance porch ties in better with the building when it does not project excessively. Recessing the doorway slightly, offers sufficient shelter by the combined depth, and casts a strong shadow, effective against light walls. This shadow also forms a background for the pattern of the ironwork.

ALLEN G. SIPLE, ARCHITECT

WILLIAM MCCAY, ARCHITECT

When garage and service wing project toward the street, the main entrance is apt to seem a minor element. In this example the two-storied porch with the splendid railing demands attention, while the path to it is made engaging by the picket fence, the lamp post, the planting and the batten wall of the wing itself.

The use of several materials will help make a facade interesting. However, to keep it from becoming spotty, one material should predominate; the whole design may be unified by an all-over color, relying upon the surface texture for variation. Wood, brick, iron and flagging are successfully combined here.

ALLEN G. SIPLE, ARCHITECT

H. ROY KELLEY, ARCHITECT

ROLAND E. COATE, ARCHITECT
YOCH AND COUNCIL, LANDSCAPE ARCHITECTS

This house is influenced by the Eighteenth Century domestic architecture of France, particularly that of the smaller houses which expressed elegance without extravagance. Yet the simplified treatment proclaims this a building of the 1930's. The slight curve of the head of the door and its repetition in the cornice above are refreshing.

This entrance shows several interesting details. The colonettes are plain round, with a couple of turnings at the top. The lattice is extremely delicate and graceful. The trim around the door carries a fine beading, and the lower panels of the door itself are no more than suggested.

The entrance door deserves careful study, for the visitor will examine it in detail while waiting for the bell to be answered. Sidelights give an opportunity to see who is at the door before opening it. The inconvenience of a step at the threshold, included in houses for cold climates to keep snow from piling up against the door, may be eliminated where a porch offers protection.

The semi-circular hood expresses the delicacy and refinement of Georgian architecture. Note how the electric fixture here is flush with the ceiling. This is a sensible location, and does not interfere with the design.

EUGENE WESTON, JR., ARCHITECT

ROLAND E. COATE, ARCHITECT
KATHERINE BASHFORD, LANDSCAPE ARCHITECT

MARSTON AND MAYBURY, ARCHITECTS

The window of a lavatory is likely to be near the front door, so it is desirable to mask it. With a brick wall interesting openwork patterns may be built in front of the window with the brick itself, seemingly a part of the wall. Since some light and air are lost by this treatment, the window should be made larger to compensate.

The kitchen window often seems ashamed of itself, and hides behind lattice and bushes, or is made smaller than desirable. Here the bank of four casements is proudly letting in as much sunshine as possible. A feature is made of it, in fact, by the break in the cornice and the shelf in front with the gourds.

GORDON B. KAUFMANN, ARCHITECT

ROLAND E. COATE, ARCHITECT
YOCH AND COUNCIL, LANDSCAPE ARCHITECTS

From a design standpoint the bay window establishes a strong center of interest; it also admits plenty of light. The narrow sides allow space for casement or double-hung windows for ventilation, an advantage over the fixed sash, flush with the wall.

GORDON B. KAUFMANN, ARCHITECT

Unity of design is gained in a bay window by using one large, fixed sash at the front. Mullions, the heavy, vertical supports, are then confined to the corners. The sides of the window on the right are deep enough to include doors leading out to the terrace.

In a city house the large, fixed sash, whether flush or in a bay window, is more useful when it opens upon a court or garden assured of privacy. Then there is no need to draw shades to block out the gaze of people on the street.

At times a simple window has an important position, and needs to be emphasized. One method is shown here. The shelf offers a convenient spot for plants, which can be watered from within. Restraint must be exercised in using such ideas, however, or the house will become a hodgepodge.

KENNETH S. WING, ARCHITECT

ALLEN G. SIPLE, ARCHITECT

26

WILLIAM WILSON WURSTER, ARCHITECT

The possibilities presented by the fixed sash are numerous. The shape is usually a plain rectangle like this first-floor sash, but it may be varied to satisfy interior conditions. This magnificent window, making a sunroom of a large second-floor hall, has been given even more glass area where the stair permits the sill to be dropped at the landing.

This room, suitable for use in warm weather, may be completely thrown open to Nature. The walls are composed of glass panels which slide, but which are entirely removable. The heavy overhang of the roof keeps out excessive sunlight without restricting the view of trees and sky.

HARWELL HAMILTON HARRIS, DESIGNER

WILLIAM WILSON WURSTER, ARCHITECT
THOMAS D. CHURCH, LANDSCAPE ARCHITECT

The exterior stair gives a pleasant supplementary communication between floors. With this hillside house it is used to join the living room with the living terrace below. In its spiral form this stair is both compact and lovely. Much of its charm comes from the handling of the wood.

WINCHTON LEAMON RISLEY, ARCHITECT

# OUTDOOR LIVING

The leisure that has been granted by the machine age is only now commencing to be enjoyed. At the same time a decided reaction from the artificiality and formality of Nineteenth Century society has taken place. These conditions have combined to develop a keen appreciation of the outdoors. This is characterized by a genuine fondness for gardens, for grass and trees, and, above all, for the sense of freedom felt in the open air.

The modern home can hardly be considered complete without some provisions being made for this outdoor life. Whether this be a simple, paved terrace or a broad, well-furnished porch, it adds appreciably to the liveable space of the house at slight additional expense. The outdoor living area of to-day is quite different from the front veranda of not so long ago. It resembles a comfortable living room which invites one outside. It is closely connected with the interior of the house by the creation of an easy passage from one to the other. Likewise, its paving merges with the lawn and garden beyond, since the first floor of to-day's house is kept close to the ground. This uninterrupted flow of space is a quality to be sought.

The location of the terrace or porch will be determined by such factors as sun, prevailing winds, view, gardens, the shape and size of the lot, and the relation of the building to the street. Privacy is usually desired. Therefore the contemporary house is very apt to open out toward the rear.

To give the greatest benefit, the outdoor living area should be readily accessible from within. A position adjacent to the hall supplies the most direct access from all parts of the house, and does not require crossing any room. On the other hand, an approach from the living room integrates these two living areas, while a way from the kitchen is convenient for serving outdoor meals. The ideal solution would combine these three.

When it is realized that most of the United States enjoys at least five months of weather suitable for out-door living, such a feature scarcely seems an extravagance. Already a part of the country house, it can do a lot to make life pleasant for the person who must spend his summers in the city.

ROLAND E. COATE, ARCHITECT
YOCH AND COUNCIL, LANDSCAPE ARCHITECTS

A delightful approach to the garden is provided here. The door from the hall opens out to a porch large enough for a grouping of furniture. The iron railing suggests a pause for a glimpse of the garden beyond. Then a turn to the left leads to the open terrace, and three steps down bring you to the lawn.

GORDON B. KAUFMANN, ARCHITECT

The good looks and comfort of the new porch furniture encourage outdoor living. The width of a porch should permit plenty of freedom in the arrangement of furniture. A generous height will give a feeling of openness, and will not deprive the rooms behind of much light or air.

Where the porch floor is extended to form an open terrace, leave areas of dirt for vines which can be trained up the posts and leaders. Being in the ground and not in pots, they will escape the frost. Flowers and shrubs in planting strips at the base of walls will soften that angle.

H. ROY KELLEY, ARCHITECT

CURTIS CHAMBERS, ARCHITECT

In a simple, unpretentious way the living room, covered porch and open terrace are here closely integrated. The large glass area and slender metal mullions serve rather to keep out the weather than to create a separation from the outdoors. The extension of the brick floor beyond the roof and the clear span between the window and corner-post throw the outdoor living area together.

A covered second-story veranda is a commanding architectural feature, but perhaps a luxury. Nevertheless, it is convenient for invalids and elderly people who cannot easily use stairs, and is a fine place for putting the baby for his nap. Its position should not be such that it darkens the windows of living rooms or bedrooms.

GORDON B. KAUFMANN, ARCHITECT

GARDNER A. DAILEY, ARCHITECT

A rambling character is often attractive, particularly for the country house. The building itself need not be unusually long; the results may be obtained by outbuildings, walls, trellises, loggias, planting. In this illustration the garage at the extreme left is detached, but is tied to the house by the solid wooden fence, which screens the service yard.

The roof of a porch may not project far from the wall, but the floor may be extended beyond the eaves to gain a comfortable width. This will protect the furniture without excessively darkening the windows beneath the roof. Then the chairs may be drawn into the sun or moved back to the shade at will.

PAUL R. WILLIAMS, ARCHITECT

CHARLES O. MATCHAM, ARCHITECT

A variation to the iron or wooden post is the brick pier. The small size of a brick allows numerous designs, simple ones being generally preferable. Exposed rafters make an interesting pattern of light and shade, and give a sense of greater height to the porch.

This terrace seems to be integral with the house, partly because the passage through the wide doorway into the living room is so easy, and partly because the main roof extends out to give some shelter. This latter treatment has here made possible the elimination of posts. The outside fireplace increases the possibilities of outdoor living, for the terrace can be made comfortable on cool evenings.

MICHAEL GOODMAN, ARCHITECT

WINCHTON LEAMON RISLEY, ARCHITECT

The location of the living terrace is influenced to a great extent by sun, view and winds. These may suggest that it be placed adjacent to the entrance of the house, a position that extends a warm welcome. On a small lot this is usually done at a sacrifice of privacy, but on a large one the only disturbance is occasioned by people arriving at the front door.

Too little thought is given to the service entrance. Usually no more is attempted than to screen it from the gaze of public, family and guests. The creation of an attractive setting where the maid or housewife may relax occasionally, particularly in these days of efficiency kitchens, is well worth the expense.

ARTHUR L. HERBERGER, ARCHITECT

WINCHTON LEAMON RISLEY, ARCHITECT

Because a patio is an inner court and enclosed on all sides, it is more intimately connected with the house than is a porch. It can be used as another room or as a means of communication. The walls make of it a harborer of the sun and a retreat from the strong winds that must be considered in certain sections of the country.

The privacy assured by high walls is another point in favor of a patio. In a closely-built community it may be the only solution to outdoor living without being disturbed by neighbors or looking at ugly backyards. A roof over part of the area is desirable.

RALPH C. FLEWELLING, ARCHITECT

GORDON B. KAUFMANN, ARCHITECT

The domestic barbecue pit is not large enough to roast an animal whole, as its name would imply. A small grill is satisfactory for the ordinary outdoor meal; in design it may be inconspicuous but handy. This shelf seems made for flower pots when not used for dishes.

Cooking on a porch or in a garden is becoming increasingly popular along with the trend towards outdoor living. A position close to the kitchen will encourage a more frequent use; supplies can be brought out more easily. Shelves nearby are useful for food, plates and utensils, avoiding the necessity of extra tables.

Where a door leads directly from the kitchen to the terrace, the serving of outdoor meals is greatly simplified. This entrance to the serving pantry of a large house has been given a certain architectural embellishment, but the advantage of easy communication has been frankly acknowledged.

SPENCER AND LANDON, ARCHITECTS

JAMES E. DOLENA, ARCHITECT

HETH WHARTON, ARCHITECT

Here advantage is taken of sloping land to develop an interesting plan. The roof is extended in one long sweep beyond the wall of the building to create on a lower level a covered area for outdoor living which seems an intimate part of the site. The long, unbroken line of the roof, accenting the slope of the land, possesses an innate beauty.

Although this is a fishing club, it suggests how a country house may take advantage of a placid water setting. What a delightful location for a porch, and how refreshing, particularly on a hot summer evening! The level of the pool or pond would have to be kept constant by a dam, spillway and water supply.

GORDON B. KAUFMANN, ARCHITECT

WINCHTON LEAMON RISLEY, ARCHITECT

Rather than foolishly pretend that a hillside lot will allow the same treatment as a level one, develop the peculiarities of the land into an asset. Here the descent to the terrace from the street is made gradual and pleasant by walls, walks and planting, at the same time assuring privacy for the outdoor living room. A quiet, sunny court is created, protected from the winds on the other side of the house.

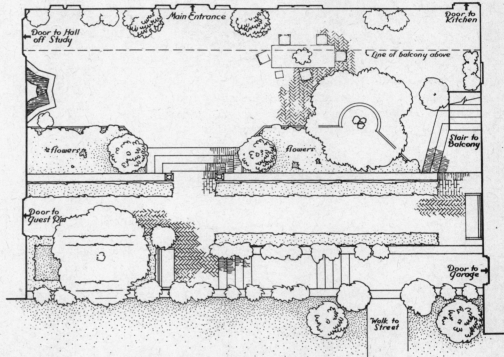

*An Out-of-Doors Living Room*

THOMAS D. CHURCH, LANDSCAPE ARCHITECT

The pot garden offers continuous bloom in a small space; when one plant has blossomed another is easily put in its place. In winter there are no barren patches of dirt. Paved terraces and masonry walls lend themselves to this treatment. The necessary daily watering is no chore when there is a pool handy for dipping the watering-pot.

One way to make a retaining wall seem lower is to build seats in front of it. These invite you to sit down outdoors whether the regular furniture is in place or not. Notice how brick is used for floor, wall and seats.

THOMAS D. CHURCH, LANDSCAPE ARCHITECT

PAUL R. WILLIAMS, ARCHITECT

The surface of a brick wall in a garden may be appropriately left rough, with little care spent on finishing the joints. A high wall is useful for screening the service quarters. A niche may be employed to accent a vista from a window as well as to develop the land more fully.

The difficult feat of treating a high retaining wall is here done in an interesting and unusual fashion. A shallow loggia divides the length into bays, which are filled with bamboo plants in tubs. A richness is given to the garden by the use of figures, which bring in both form and color. The railing and posts are redwood, treated with boiled linseed oil.

WINFIELD SCOTT WELLINGTON, ARCHITECT

ROLAND E. COATE, ARCHITECT
YOCH AND COUNCIL, LANDSCAPE ARCHITECTS

A formal, symmetrical design demands a similar landscaping treatment. The flower garden, though related to the house, is kept at a distance by a broad lawn area which acts as a setting for the architecture. Trees are effective for framing a building. Their heavy foliage will provide additional shaded places for outdoor living.

The relation of the garden to the house is important. To establish a bond, paths and steps may be centered on architectural features as bay windows, doors or walls rather than be terminated hit-or-miss. This treatment thus presents interesting objects at the ends of vistas.

ROLAND E. COATE, ARCHITECT
KATHERINE BASHFORD, LANDSCAPE ARCHITECT

The circular brick steps in the foreground lead from the house terrace; those beyond to the flower walk which surrounds the rectangular lawn terrace in the middle. This composition is repeated on the left to form a symmetrical design. The brick edging at the base of the sloping wall is flush with the grass, and supplies a neat cutting line.

Psychologically, a few steps up-grade seem more tiring than twice that many down. For that reason, when the lawn or garden is above the level of the terrace, the steps must be made extremely attractive and gentle.

44

WILLIAM WILSON WURSTER, ARCHITECT
THOMAS D. CHURCH, LANDSCAPE ARCHITECT

Wood lends itself to innumerable variations in the design of fences, walls and railings. The forms here fulfil admirably their respective functions, but are not weighted down with superfluous ornament. Their loveliness comes from the studied relation between voids and solids. Flower beds have been included as an edging, the only place near the house that such a steep lot offered.

Brick, stone and concrete are substantial materials for walls, but are likely to be costly. Wood is usually just as satisfactory for a screen, and is a splendid medium for paint to gain color. Here the boards are of redwood laid horizontally with flush joints. The wall and tree together provide a delightful, secluded terrace for summer meals.

THOMAS D. CHURCH, LANDSCAPE ARCHITECT

WILLIAM WILSON WURSTER, ARCHITECT

# THE INTERIOR

It is the interior of the house with which the owner comes into closest contact, so it is here that conveni-ence has the most appeal. It is here that a fine consideration of details will have direct bearing on the success of the finished building.

Up until recently a house was little more than a series of box-like rooms. To-day all sorts of accommoda-tions are included also. Built-in furniture plays an important role in the logical approach to a comfortable home. Windows and doors are placed where they are the most beneficial. Closets are not just so much space; their position, size and equipment are carefully thought out.

This desire for convenience has been accompanied by a fresher and cleaner handling of the design. No longer is profuse elaboration considered smart. It clutters up the interior, whereas broad smooth surfaces tend to open it up. This latter quality makes it easier to keep the contemporary house free of dust. This trend toward sim-plicity is more than a cyclical reaction. The cost of labor is now so high that it is necessary to reduce to a mini-mum all handwork in construction.

**46**    The increased cost of building, together with the added expense of including both the necessary mechanical improvements and the refinements of modern planning, severely limits the size of a house. This situation has resulted in the elimination of some partitions. For instance, a large living room with a place for dining is likely to be preferred to two small stuffy rooms, and is obviously less expensive than supplying a separate adequate dining room. While provision is still made for proper performance of the functions of a household, the areas where they occur are less rigidly defined.

The outstanding characteristic of to-day, however, is the growth of a liberal attitude toward the creation of a home. This promises even finer things to come. No longer is there a taboo against any detail that caters to the owner's comfort and enjoyment, so long as it is pleasantly incorporated in the finished design. It is a static form of architecture indeed that fails to make provision for the living customs of to-day.

HARWELL HAMILTON HARRIS, DESIGNER

When one wall of a room is composed of glass panels that slide back, the room may be opened in favorable weather on to a terrace, appreciably increasing its size. A solid wall beyond permits such an arrangement even with neighbors close at hand, and walls on the two sides assure seclusion for each room.

HERVEY PARKE CLARK, ARCHITECT

The trend toward simplicity in domestic architecture is as evident on the interior of the house as it is on the exterior. The warmth and calmness of this room are due mainly to the care bestowed on form and color, and to the ceiling of unpainted redwood boards. The extra thickness of the wall on the left, containing the chimney, wood box and bookshelves, prevents the French doors from projecting into the room.

The subdued handling of this library is praiseworthy. It is as true in architecture as in other fields that the simple but satisfying result which seems so easy is really the most difficult to achieve. For an example of this elimination of unnecessary detail, notice that the curtain box is made a part of the wall surface.

H. ROY KELLEY, ARCHITECT

H. ROY KELLEY, ARCHITECT

A room may be designed to serve as a sympathetic background for antique furniture, and yet not be a slavish imitation of a period style. The extensive glass area on the right with the French doors leading to the porch is a solution dictated by contemporary living customs. Notice also the wood curtain box flush with the wall.

Spaciousness is particularly appropriate for the country house. It may be obtained economically by throwing entrance hall, living room, dining room and even study together into one large area. Height may be acquired by omitting a ceiling, and exposing the rafters and the underside of the roof sheathing.

HETH WHARTON, ARCHITECT

ROLAND E. COATE, ARCHITECT

One of the charms of vertical boarding is the number of variations obtainable with the joints. Although the stock beaded and v-jointed mouldings are often satisfactory, you may select your own at little if any extra cost. The mantle formed of an architrave moulding is the simplest method of covering the joint between the brick facing of a fireplace and the wall surface. It may be emphasized by a cornice member which will also serve as a shelf.

Houses have grown so small that the guest room is actually a luxury, and must be dispensed with at times. In this living room the window-seat has been made almost the size of a double bed to care for the occasional guest. Notice also that the top of the desk can fold up into the wall and out of the way.

CHARLES O. MATCHAM, ARCHITECT

H. ROY KELLEY, ARCHITECT

Bookshelves must be provided in practically all homes. The effect is better if they are built in and included in the architectural treatment rather than installed later as individual pieces of furniture. With a chimney on an inside wall a pleasing group may be had by placing shelves on each side of the mantle.

Another good place for bookshelves is on each side of a doorway, with the shelving extending from opening to walls. The wide door jambs are pleasant. This disposition is of special value where an added thickness of the wall is needed to prevent a step or two from projecting into the room. Notice the slat blinds in the deep window recess.

EDGAR BISSANTZ, ARCHITECT

EDGAR BISSANTZ, ARCHITECT

Where books are really enjoyed, and are not intended primarily for decorative value, a window near the shelves is helpful for reading the titles, while a window seat assures a cozy and convenient spot for reading the books. Cupboards under the shelves provide the necessary storage facilities for the overflow of books and odds and ends.

Where space for a great many books must be found, the suggestion of a tapestry is obtained by massing them in one large area. This avoids a spotty effect. Carrying the shelving practically to the floor not only completes the mass effect, but provides space for additional books.

HARWELL HAMILTON HARRIS, DESIGNER

In this library the spirit and even the general forms of the Georgian style are reproduced, but the effect is gained in a contemporary manner, without recourse to excessive detailing.

Ceilings are generally plastered, painted a light color and forgotten; but wood is a material that permits delightful results. Joists and beams, expressing the construction, may be part of the design. The settling of the house will not develop cracks later as with plaster.

Even though your stock of books is not large at present, shelves may be built and decorated in the meantime with the little ornaments that are so tempting to buy. From time to time the collection may be varied. Shelves flanking a window give adequate depth for a curtain pocket, and yet are not deep enough to cut off light.

Shelves of glass may be successfully placed between window jambs and aligned with the muntins. However, the depth of the jamb must be sufficient to care for them. This will require a thickening of the usual frame wall, or a projection of the window casing beyond the exterior wall surface. The French doors open upon a covered terrace.

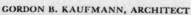

EDGAR BISSANTZ, ARCHITECT

A study is intended as a retreat from the rest of the house, as a place for keeping books and papers, and as an office. Its personal nature does not require much clear floor area, but its demands for storage must be carefully considered. Built-in facilities, including the necessary desk, will efficiently employ the space available.

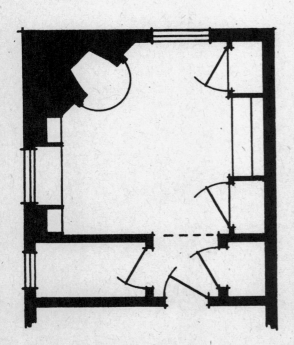

GORDON B. KAUFMANN, ARCHITECT

The generous glass area of a bay window will be enjoyed in the dining room. Most of the day you may be too busy to sit down and delight in your surroundings, but meals should be taken leisurely. A low sill will give a larger view of the outdoors, and a wide one will supply a place for plants.

Although the separate entrance hall, living room and dining room are retained in this house, the wide openings create the spaciousness that is favored today. Likewise, the elimination of superfluous detail and the use of broad, flat surfaces not only supply a restful background for the furniture, but noticeably simplify the housecleaning.

GARDNER A. DAILEY, ARCHITECT

RICHARD J. NEUTRA, ARCHITECT
PETER PFISTERER, COLLABORATOR

An alcove off the living room offers a suitable place for the dining table, and develops a vista across the combined length, but still keeps a certain segregation. To indicate a variation in use, the walls of the alcove may be papered or painted differently from the living room, and the ceiling may be dropped.

Folding doors with lattice offer a compromise between the separate dining room and the dining alcove. The circulation of air and light is not impeded, and a feeling of openness is retained, but the dining table is sufficiently screened when the doors are closed. A tile floor is cool-looking, easy to keep clean, and adds character to a room.

SPENCER AND LANDON, ARCHITECTS

CHARLES O. MATCHAM, ARCHITECT

Although the bay window cannot completely accommodate the dining furniture as an alcove does, it permits a distinct grouping that does not conflict with the arrangement of the living room pieces. Regular dining room furniture may be used without seeming incongruous. Notice that the return of the bay window is simulated by a mirror door opening on a closet.

For entering the garden a pair of narrow doors is more inviting than a single wide one. They may open into a reveal of a bay, and so not project into the room or use valuable wall space when folded back against the wall. A splendid spot for plants is provided when the corners are boxed in and covered with tile.

CHARLES O. MATCHAM, ARCHITECT

DONALD BEACH KIRBY, ARCHITECT

Corner cupboards need not be elaborate affairs exclusively for heirloom china. In their traditional location in the dining room they offer a sensible place for keeping everyday pieces.

Here is a corner cupboard with the lines of today, although reminiscent of its Colonial counterpart in general form. When a cupboard is to be used for the display of cherished pieces, a door will protect them from damage and dust, but it does tend to obscure them.

Although it is still not considered good planning to use the dining room for circulation, the freer living today, together with the lighter and more adaptable furniture obtainable, suggests that a space may serve for both dining and passageway when the house isn't run too rigidly.

DONALD BEACH KIRBY, ARCHITECT

CHARLES O. MATCHAM, ARCHITECT

CHARLES O. MATCHAM, ARCHITECT

Suitable storage space for table linen, silver and china may be obtained by building such facilities against the wall of the dining room. For many houses a tile or linoleum floor will be preferable to a carpet or rug. Food spilled can be easily removed without leaving spots.

Cupboards with solid doors may be used instead of open shelving for storage purposes in the dining room. Objects of any sort may be kept there without regard to grouping, but the decorative value of beautiful pieces is lost. A center window recessed between two such cupboards is a good solution for one wall.

ROBERT H. AINSWORTH, ARCHITECT

HARWELL HAMILTON HARRIS, DESIGNER

A generous amount of window area over sink and work space gives a feeling of spaciousness and airiness to the small kitchen. Artificial illumination is supplied by three forty-watt bulbs behind the ground glass panels over the sink, so that the cook does not work in her own shadow.

Kitchens are such standardized workshops today that it is refreshing to find one with character as well as efficiency. The little shelves with flower-pots soften the starkness of rows of cabinets. Color is introduced by the wallpaper and rubber tile. The extra height gained by exposing the rafters, possible with the one-story house, gives a delightful airiness.

ALLEN G. SIPLE, ARCHITECT

RICHARD J. NEUTRA, ARCHITECT
PETER PFISTERER, COLLABORATOR

With weatherstripping, insulation, double glazing and automatic heat, glass may be used more freely today than in Colonial times. The window can now be considered an area and not a hole punched in the wall. On dull days the interior will be bright; on sunny ones curtains or blinds can be drawn to keep out excessive sunlight. Here the projection on the exterior above the door cuts off some of the direct rays of the noonday sun.

A new field of possibilities opens up when windows are considered as masses of wall area. They may have high sills and run to the ceiling when needed only for light; they may extend to the floor where there is a view. Even a small area may be placed at the head of a sofa for reading.

R. M. SCHINDLER, ARCHITECT

RICHARD J. NEUTRA, ARCHITECT
PETER PFISTERER, COLLABORATOR

This is almost the ultimate in windows. In fact, to take advantage of mountain scenery, the window has become a wall of plate glass and narrow aluminum mullions. Light is controlled by Venetian blinds, ventilation by openings in the wall under the window. Fixed sashes are particularly appropriate for the house with all-year air conditioning.

To give the feeling that the room is thrown open to the outdoors beyond, a fixed sash extending from floor to ceiling is most satisfactory. Use a corner window if a view requires one, considering it as a unit. Metal will allow a more delicate treatment of the sash than wood.

CEDRIC GIBBONS, ART DIRECTION
METRO-GOLDWYN-MAYER PRODUCTION, "AFTER THE THIN MAN"

WILLIAM WILSON WURSTER, ARCHITECT

Special needs bring about special developments, whence comes the personality of a house. This fireplace was placed at the end of the room to diminish an unfavorable view ahead, and at the same time to force a recognition of the magnificent scenery at the two corners. The arrangement also shows how corner windows can solve the problem of lighting the end of a room when a fireplace is centered on the narrow wall.

Note here how the window completely fills the area between the brick wall on the left and the fireplace. Thus the corner of the room is extremely usable, for it is bright and cheerful, so it may be used for a grouping of furniture. This type of window should be treated as a single element bending around the corner. The curtain box helps supply the effect.

ROBERT H. AINSWORTH, ARCHITECT

WILLIAM WILSON WURSTER, ARCHITECT

The brick floor repeating that of the terrace, and the wall of flush siding recalling the exterior wall surface, give to this gallery the atmosphere of an open loggia. The glazed sash offers the necessary protection against the weather and intruders. Access to the terrace is gained by French doors in two of the bays, while ventilation is provided by in-swinging casements in the narrow sections.

The collector of glass will appreciate the perfect setting offered by rows of shelves built against windows for exhibiting the prized items. The flower-lover can create a miniature greenhouse with potted plants on the shelves. Such uses are particularly successful for the entrance vestibule, hall, or long gallery, and will not then confuse the decorative scheme of a room.

ALLEN G. SIPLE, ARCHITECT

**64**

JAMES E. DOLENA, ARCHITECT

A room not much larger than a bathroom can be developed into a cheerful and comfortable bar. Then the living room will not be thrown into disorder when drinks are served, and the furniture will not be marred by damp glasses. The garish decorations sometimes used to force a note of gaiety serve rather to produce a restlessness that detracts from good fellowship.

There is no good reason for the bar to be relegated to the cellar. Where there is plenty of natural light, drinking will be pleasanter, and probably less heavy. At a round or octagonal bar people can see each other, and are not strung out in a line. It also means fewer steps for the "bartender."

Where a separate room is impractical, a bar may be built into a closet off the living room or study, so that it can be concealed when not in use. A small refrigerator, a sink, plenty of cupboards, shelving and working surface are the requisites of a good bar. A linoleum or rubber tile floor will be helpful.

JAMES E. DOLENA, ARCHITECT

HONNOLD AND RUSSELL, ARCHITECTS

EDGAR BISSANTZ, ARCHITECT

There are so many details to consider in the building of a house that some are taken for granted. Doors, however, should be selected with care, consideration being given to the panel treatment if flush or batten doors are not to be used. Double doors allow a wider opening, and look particularly well when a pocket is built to receive them as is done here.

EDGAR BISSANTZ, ARCHITECT

Special conditions like this doorway deserve particular attention. The curve of the wall, the trim, the wooden head-piece and the termination of the dado are all matters that had to be worked out by the architect to attain a finished appearance.

The doorway with a conventional trim may be given distinction by the application of a stock moulding at the head to form a pediment. A good looking dado, which will dress up a room, is had by laying wide boards horizontally around the room, and capping them by a chair rail.

A feature may be made of a doorway by incorporating in its design a row of shelves on each side. The importance of this position in a formal room suggests that the shelves be filled with fine bindings and small objects, reserving the real books for a more intimate place.

ALLEN G. SIPLE, ARCHITECT

FURNISHED BY BARKER BROS.

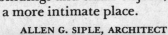

GARDNER A. DAILEY, ARCHITECT

Because this second-floor stair hall takes the form of a narrow gallery, the two halls seem as one, developing an agreeable spaciousness. The splendid window enhances this effect. This treatment is especially appropriate for this hillside house, for the front door leads to the stair landing between floors, and the window capitalizes the lovely view.

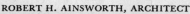

This is an open-string stair, for the treads and risers extend beyond the balusters so that their outline is visible from the side. The simple turned balusters and newel are consistent with the informal character of the wide boards with beaded joints used for the wall.

ROBERT H. AINSWORTH, ARCHITECT

PAUL R. WILLIAMS, ARCHITECT

Although retaining the form of a traditional Colonial stairway, the architect here has imparted a freshness to the design. The balusters are sturdy, but the delicate fluting gives them grace.

This is called a closed-string stair, for the treads and risers butt against the string, and are not visible from the side. The use of an open or closed string is a matter of choice; no practical considerations are involved. Handrail, balusters and newel may be slender, and delicate when made of metal.

ARCADIA, H. ROY KELLEY, ARCHITECT

WILLIAM McCAY, ARCHITECT

A window on the stairway is of great value for lighting the steps and thus preventing accidents. This railing is a successful and interesting solution. The effect of a rail fence is obtained by the substitution of the sloping members for the customary balusters.

DONALD BEACH KIRBY, ARCHITECT

When the direction of a stair changes, it is better for safety to install a platform or landing as shown here than to use radiating treads, known as winders. The ship's bell above the railing is the doorbell, and is wired so that it rings two bells.

As a background for a collection of Oriental Art, white cedar boards with inverted battens have been used extensively here. Every effort has been made to bring out the beauty of the grain of the wood. The stair rail has been developed into an interesting and original design.

This is another pattern for a wood railing in the same house as the example above. The short flight of stairs is made quite attractive by the inclusion of a balcony in the lower room. This is especially desirable when the entrance is made to a large, high room; one can stop and survey what lies below.

WINFIELD SCOTT WELLINGTON, ARCHITECT

WINFIELD SCOTT WELLINGTON, ARCHITECT

Rather than hunt for space within the walls for closets, build them out into the room like this to the depth of two feet, which is adequate for a pole and clothes-hangers. For the double room two closets with dressing table between is an ideal solution. Double doors give access to the whole closet, and louvred doors provide a circulation of air within, although they also admit dust.

Here again practical closets are incorporated in the design of a bedroom wall. This treatment is emphasized by the use of boards with beaded joints in contrast to the plaster on the other walls. The room is wide enough so that the doors can open into the alcove, permitting furniture to be placed against the sides of the closets.

CHARLES O. MATCHAM, ARCHITECT

GARDNER A. DAILEY, ARCHITECT

One half of the interior of this closet is occupied by sliding trays, the other by a shelf and a pole for coat-hangers. Flush doors have no mouldings to collect dust. The window seat not only squares up this end of the room, but has storage space underneath its hinged covers. The bed and bedside table are also built in.

Perhaps the most purely personal luxury a house can possess is a spacious owner's bedroom, one that will even accommodate a sofa and easy chair without crowding. A fireplace will add a restful note, but should be included only where the size of the room warrants it. The bedroom can then serve as an upstairs sitting room.

H. ROY KELLEY, ARCHITECT

EDGAR BISSANTZ, ARCHITECT

Built-in furniture is of special value for the small room. Each piece is accurately sized beforehand, and then related to the others; no waste space is left between them to collect dust. The resulting concentration of all unused floor area makes the room appear larger. The employment of a few plain surfaces easily accessible lightens the housework.

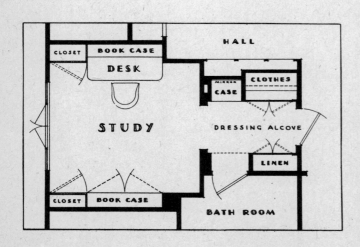

Here is another dressing table between two closets at the end of a bedroom. The window is ideally located for lighting your face during the day. At night a lamp is handy, but the illumination would have been improved by one on the right also. The electric outlet in the knee space is useful. The round mirror and those at the sides are clear glass; the table top and back are blue.

ALLEN G. SIPLE, ARCHITECT

HERTZKA AND KNOWLES, ARCHITECTS
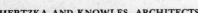

Here are exhibited a number of features that you will want for your bathroom. The tile counters give an ample, dry surface for placing toilet articles, obviating the necessity of balancing them on the narrow, wet rim of the ordinary free-standing lavatory. The fine cupboards and drawers below are ideal for storage of large bottles, soap and brushes among other things. The stall shower with frosted glass door is not only much pleasanter to use than a shower spray over a tub, but also reduces the hazard of slipping. The three-part mirror and Lumiline lamp speak for themselves, and the electric heater will be a delight on cool mornings.

72

MICHAEL GOODMAN, ARCHITECT

# HOUSES WITH PLANS

In the three previous sections the aim has been to present the details that are the basis of the liveable and practical house. Here by means of plans it is hoped to show how these elements may be coordinated into a harmonious building. This involves a consideration of such larger aspects of planning as the relative position of rooms, the communication between them, orientation and the characteristics of the site.

The connection between the house and its lot is so important that the landscaping treatment has been included wherever possible. A plan of the grounds should be made for every house to assure a pleasant location for the outdoor living area, and to provide easy passage between the drive, garage, and house. Other points that should be taken into account are a proper setting for the building, open lawn areas, flower and vegetable gardens, a play space and a service yard.

The descriptive outline is presented so that it may be easier to visualize each house. At the same time it serves as a check-list of materials that furnish the finished appearance. The exterior color scheme has been noted as well. While color is now an important part of the interior decoration of a home, the many opportunities it offers for the exterior are too often ignored. It is an economical medium with which to gain distinctive effects.

Costs have been supplied when they were available. They are helpful, but they must be employed with discretion. It is well to remember that prices vary for different parts of the country, that they change from month to month, and that they are appreciably affected by the specifications and equipment.

These plans are offered as guides to the solution of the many problems involved in building. While it is hoped that each will contain ideas that are useful, it is not intended that any one should be copied in its entirety. Considering them in this broader aspect will make them of greater value to the person planning a home. Then he can freely develop a plan suitable to his own tastes and his own requirements.

WILLIAM WILSON WURSTER, ARCHITECT

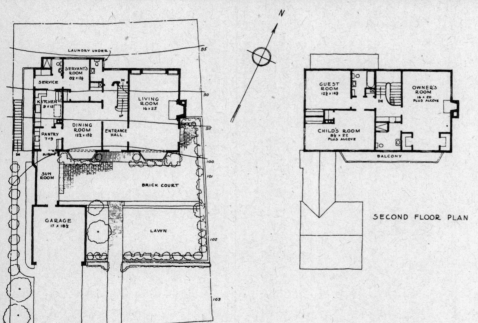

FIRST FLOOR PLAN

SECOND FLOOR PLAN

## DESCRIPTIVE OUTLINE

### EXTERIOR

| | |
|---|---|
| WALLS | Cement plaster |
| ROOF | Cedar shingles |
| WINDOWS | Wood, double hung and casement |
| COLOR | Walls, trim and doors— oyster white. Roof—natural. |

### INTERIOR

| | |
|---|---|
| FLOORS | Living rooms, bedrooms and halls—oak. Kitchen and baths— linoleum. |
| WALLS | Wallpaper in dining room. Plaster elsewhere. |
| CEILINGS | Plaster. |
| LIGHTING | A minimum of fixtures. Mostly by table lamps. |
| CUBAGE | 3,515 square feet or approximately 38,000 cubic feet. |

With some city lots the outdoor living area must be near the street. In this example, the front half of the lot is fairly flat, but the rear falls off steeply to the north. To preserve as much of this level area as possible, the house has been placed towards the rear, and to gain a secluded area, an intimate walled forecourt has been created. This is also the sunny side of the house. Such a treatment screens the large bay windows from the road. What might have been simply a passage from the garage to the house has been widened a bit to make of it a delightful sun room which is completely hidden from the street, protected from the winds and well located for outdoor meals. To obtain access to the outside from the living room and yet not disturb the grouping of furniture around the bay window, the brick terrace has been carried along the side far enough to allow a door. The intrinsic beauty attainable with a quiet and simple handling is well illustrated here.

Entrance detail shown on page 12.

SPENCER AND LANDON, ARCHITECTS

## DESCRIPTIVE OUTLINE

### EXTERIOR

WALLS     Stucco

ROOF     Wood shingle

WINDOWS     Steel casement

COLOR     Walls—off-white with buff dado
Roof—natural
Trim, blinds and doors —off-white

### INTERIOR

FLOORS     Living room and dining room—12"x12" red Placio tile
Bedrooms and hall —oak
Kitchen—linoleum
Baths—tile

WALLS     Study—wood paneling
Living room and dining room—wood and plaster
Bedrooms and halls— plaster
Kitchen and baths— tile and Sanitas

CEILINGS     Living rooms and bedrooms—exposed wood roof framing
Halls, kitchen and baths—plaster

LIGHTING     Direct

AREA     2,580 square feet

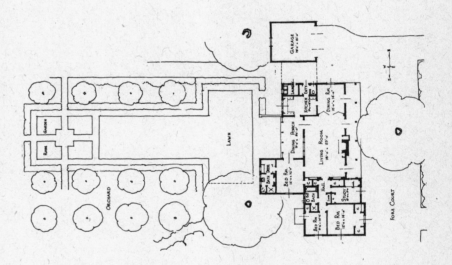

The one-story house not only presents a long, low mass suggestive of domesticity and tranquillity, but is suitable to the organic planning appropriate for to-day's living. The plan is able to express the pleasures and habits of the owner and his family, and need not be moulded into a preconceived geometrical form. For example, the arrangement of the bedrooms is not confined to the outline of a first floor, and their sizes are not determined by partitions below. With everything on one floor it is easier to get about the house, so the work is simplified. Just the elimination of stairs may be a deciding factor in the selection of a one-story house. They are a nuisance, a danger, a handicap to invalids, and a strain to those with weak hearts. With all rooms close to the ground, the building establishes an intimate contact with the site, and bedrooms as well as living rooms may open out to terraces and gardens.

The one-story house is practical for the city lot as well as for acreage in the country. Care must be exercised, however, that all rooms have plenty of light and air, that some way is provided to reach the garden, that there is sufficient separation of activities, and that long, narrow corridors are not necessary.

Living room shown on page 55.

KENNETH S. WING, ARCHITECT

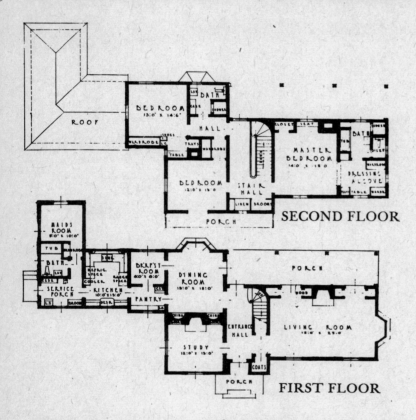

SECOND FLOOR

FIRST FLOOR

The architect has not only provided an eminently satisfactory plan for this house, but has managed to include almost every possible convenience that an owner could desire. From the front door there is a vista through the entrance hall to the two-story porch beyond. Living room, dining room and study are entered directly from the hall. The dining room supplies space for furniture on the center of its walls as a result of the consideration given to the placing of the doors. The kitchen is bright, has cross ventilation, a work space free from traffic passing through the room, and a desk.

The second-floor hall is cheerful with its window; long, dark corridors have been avoided. Where a bath serves two bedrooms, it is better that it be entered from a subsidiary hall, as here, than directly from each room. Greater privacy is secured for the bath, and there is no danger that a door be left locked when the bath is vacant. Especially where a separate lavatory is not included, you should be able to enter one bath from the hall. The bedrooms illustrate the wisdom of keeping the beds in mind when planning. Good wall space is provided. Also the doors are concentrated, so that the need of walking around three sides of a bed to go from one to another is eliminated.

## DESCRIPTIVE OUTLINE

### EXTERIOR

| | |
|---|---|
| WALLS | Cement plaster |
| ROOF | Cedar shingles |
| WINDOWS | Wood, double hung |
| COLOR | Walls and trim—off-white<br>Roof—black<br>Blinds—blue-green |

### INTERIOR

| | |
|---|---|
| FLOORS | Living rooms, bedrooms and halls—oak<br>Breakfast room and service rooms—linoleum<br>Baths—tile and linoleum |
| WALLS | Living rooms, bedrooms and halls—wallpaper<br>Kitchen—Sanitas |
| CEILINGS | Plaster, painted |
| LIGHTING | Direct |
| CUBAGE | 55,543 cubic feet |

ROLAND E. COATE, ARCHITECT; YOCH AND COUNCIL, LANDSCAPE ARCHITECTS

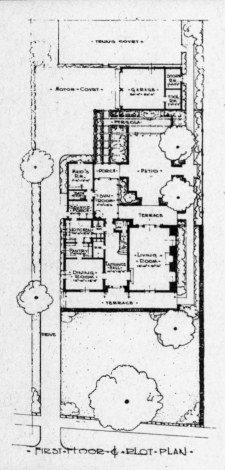

- FIRST-FLOOR-&-PLOT-PLAN -

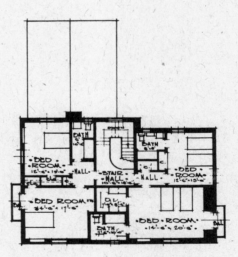

- SECOND - FLOOR - PLAN -

## DESCRIPTIVE OUTLINE
### EXTERIOR
WALLS     Cement plaster

ROOF     Shakes

WINDOWS     Wood, double hung

COLOR     Walls, trim and doors—
white
Roof—natural
Blinds—dark

The brick terrace with its boxwood edging extending across the whole facade and the broad front lawn panel uncut by a center walk are two factors contributing to the feeling of stability and dignity offered by this house. From the practical standpoint, the terrace gives access to the drive on one side, and connects with a path to the patio or garden and tennis court on the other. Where there is sufficient privacy, such a terrace may be used for outdoor living.

The plan has a center hall. The stairs are placed at the rear, where a window can light them. The telephone room is handy for the family, and assures a quiet spot. At the same time it is convenient for the maid to answer calls. Four large bedrooms, each with cross ventilation, and three bathrooms are provided for the second floor, often a difficult task with this type of plan.

Entrance terrace shown on page 10.

ALLEN G. SIPLE, ARCHITECT

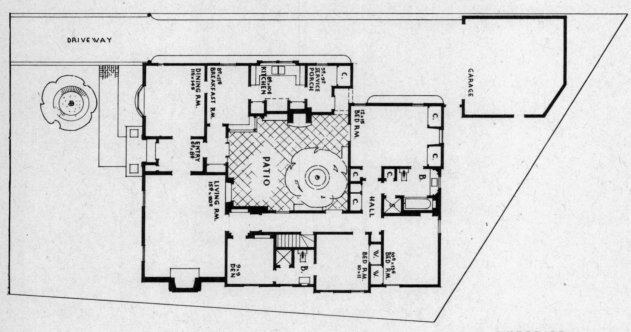

A patio or court that is enclosed on all sides by walls, but open above, is not always satisfactory. In some localities it is likely to be hot in the summer, for breezes are cut off. In cold climates it forms a snow pocket, and makes heating difficult. Yet it does possess definite advantages, and need not be summarily dismissed. Primarily it assures a privacy for outdoor living and a sheltered play space for children, both of which are difficult to provide on a small lot in a closely built district. It also allows the development of a more open plan, which results in better light and cross ventilation for rooms and halls. The important consideration with a patio is to make it sufficiently large so that it will not be an ugly damp light-court.

Dressing table shown on page 71.

**EXTERIOR**

| | |
|---|---|
| WALLS | Brick veneer and stucco |
| ROOF | Cedar shingles |
| WINDOWS | Wood, double hung |
| COLOR | Walls, trim and blinds —white |
| | Roof—grey |

**INTERIOR**

| | |
|---|---|
| FLOORS | Living rooms, bed-rooms and halls—oak Baths—tile and linoleum |
| WALLS | Wallpaper and painted canvas |
| CEILINGS | Painted |

EARL WEBSTER AND ADRIAN WILSON, ARCHITECTS

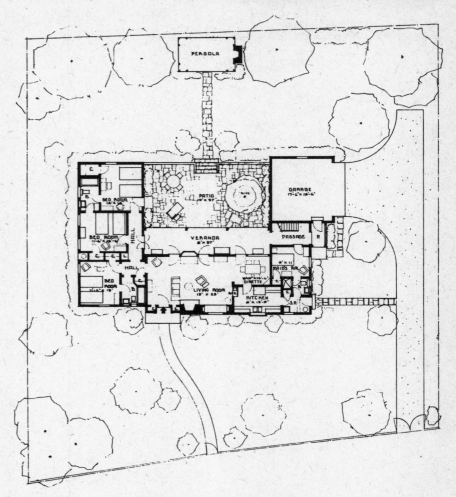

## DESCRIPTIVE OUTLINE

### EXTERIOR

WALLS     Stucco. Vertical redwood boarding at entry, veranda and garage

ROOF     Clay shingle tile with thin white glaze

WINDOWS     Steel casement

COLOR     Walls, roof, trim and doors—off-white
Blinds—blue-green

### INTERIOR

FLOORS     Living rooms, bedrooms and halls—cement with integral color
Kitchen and baths—asphalt tile

WALLS     Plaster, painted

CEILINGS     Living rooms, bedrooms and halls—1"x6" wood plank, painted
Kitchen and baths—plaster, painted

CUBAGE     22,000 cubic feet

The mass of a garage may be advantageously employed to give direction to a plan. A number of the houses shown in this book derive, in an economical manner, their rambling and spacious character from its well-considered disposition. In this example the house proper is L-shaped, but the garage is used to form a U-shaped plan, providing a protected patio. The passage, which further extends this wing, allows guests to enter the patio from the drive without the bother of passing through the house. This type of plan supplies much sunlight, and gives access to the outdoor area from all rooms.

The specifications show how carefully the architects have considered the situation of this house on the desert. Floors are of cement to eliminate the termite hazard, steel sashes are used throughout to prevent the excessive shrinkage experienced with wood sash in such a dry atmosphere, and the roof is covered with shingle tile glazed a grey-white to reflect the heat of the sun.

WINCHTON LEAMON RISLEY, ARCHITECT

FIRST FLOOR PLAN

SECOND FLOOR PLAN

## DESCRIPTIVE OUTLINE

### EXTERIOR

| | |
|---|---|
| WALLS | Cement plaster and redwood siding |
| ROOF | Wood shingles |
| WINDOWS | Wood, double hung |
| COLOR | Walls—two shades of yellow with henna dado at rear porch<br>Roof—dark<br>Trim and blinds—white<br>Sash—yellow |

### INTERIOR

| | |
|---|---|
| FLOORS | Living rooms, bedrooms and halls—oak<br>Breakfast room, kitchen and laundry—linoleum<br>Baths—tile |
| WALLS | Living rooms, breakfast room, bedrooms and halls—wallpaper<br>Kitchen and laundry—painted canvas<br>Baths—Sanitas |
| CEILINGS | Living rooms, breakfast room, bedrooms and halls—plaster, kalsomined<br>Kitchen, laundry and baths—painted canvas |
| LIGHTING | Brass fixtures |
| CUBAGE | 35,653 cubic feet |

In the design of this house particular attention has been paid to providing outdoor areas for meals and recreation protected from the prevailing winds. This has resulted in a delightfully private patio overlooking the orchard. The porch with doors from living room, hall, dining room and breakfast room coordinates this treatment. In the design of the garage provision has been made for the storage of trunks, fuel and tools, and a covered way connects it with the breakfast room. The kitchen is arranged so that the circulation through it does not cut across the work center by the sink.

By placing the maid's room near the kitchen, her quarters are effectively separated from the family's. The service stair can then be eliminated, for it would be used but little. Such a location also helps in the running of the house, for, even though resting in the afternoon, the maid can have an eye out for any long cooking operation, can easily answer the front door and telephone, and is at hand to receive deliveries at the service door. Her room should open from a service porch or hall, and not directly from the kitchen.

WILLIAM WILSON WURSTER, ARCHITECT

## DESCRIPTIVE OUTLINE

### EXTERIOR

**WALLS**     Cement plaster

**ROOF**     Tar and gravel. "Lay-kold" deck

**WINDOWS**     Wood, double hung. Steel, fixed sash and casement

**COLOR**     Center block of house—clay color
Elsewhere—linen color
Roll blinds in sun room—green

### INTERIOR

**FLOORS**     Entry and living, guest, owner's and girl's rooms—oak
Children's bath—tile
Elsewhere—linoleum

**WALLS**     Study and boy's room—Douglas fir plywood
Elsewhere—plaster

**CEILINGS**     Study and boy's room—Douglas fir plywood
Elsewhere—plaster

**LIGHTING**     A minimum of fixtures. A few flush ceiling boxes. Mostly by table lamps

**CUBAGE**     3,036 square feet or approximately 33,000 cubic feet

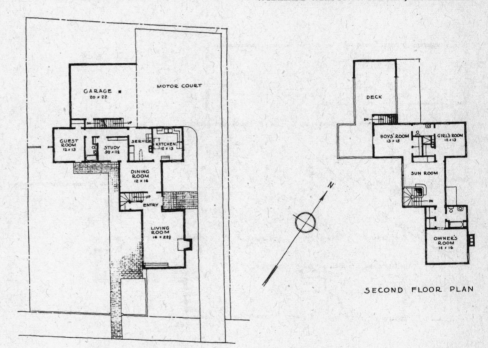

FIRST FLOOR PLAN

SECOND FLOOR PLAN

The design of this house has not been influenced by any historic style. The walls and roof have been treated essentially as a shell for enclosing space, and the windows as a means of providing light and ventilation. Nevertheless the architect has not been content with only these practical considerations, but has carefully studied the proportions of each element, and has combined them into a most pleasing whole.

The placing of the windows is particularly successful. Their position has been influenced by the need for wide wall surfaces for furniture, especially in the bedrooms. However, they have not been arbitrarily located without regard to their appearance on the exterior.

The sun room on the second floor, lighted by the great window, is a bright and cheery spot. Although seemingly good-sized, it has been obtained simply by enlarging the hall slightly. Here it makes a fine playroom for the children, but such an arrangement may be used for an upstairs sitting room, or it may be included just for the joy of having a spacious hall.

Sun room window shown on page 27.

KENNETH S. WING, ARCHITECT

FLOOR PLAN

## DESCRIPTIVE OUTLINE

### EXTERIOR

| | |
|---|---|
| WALLS | Cement plaster |
| ROOF | Cedar shingles |
| WINDOWS | Wood, double hung |
| COLOR | Walls and trim—off-white<br>Roof—natural<br>Blinds—blue-green |

### INTERIOR

| | |
|---|---|
| FLOORS | Living rooms, bedrooms and halls—oak<br>Kitchen—linoleum<br>Baths—linoleum and tile |
| WALLS | Living rooms, bedrooms and halls—wallpaper<br>Kitchen—Sealex wall covering |
| CEILINGS | Painted |
| LIGHTING | Direct |
| CUBAGE | 36,000 cubic feet |

The accommodations offered by this house are both various and liberal, but they have been organized harmoniously so that the exterior shows a desirable unity and restraint. The wall surfaces are plain; the roof areas, broad and simple. The calmness of the whole is helped by the fenestration; a uniform size was selected for the windows, so that they become a part of the general scheme, and do not vie with one another for attention. Thus, although the porch with its recessed doorway is treated in an unpretentious manner, it is inviting and able to hold the eye.

The plan is particularly expressive of a corner lot. The bedrooms project on the front to screen the entrance porch from the next house. The wing extending along the side street is not only the desirable location for service and garage, but at the same time develops a protected outdoor living area off the living room. The bedroom next to the dining room is intended for a maid, and is located so that it will not be too far from the child's room. The use of wardrobes with sliding doors in the dressing room and child's room permits an efficient use of closet space.

Dining room window shown on page 26.

KEMPER NOMLAND, ARCHITECT

## DESCRIPTIVE OUTLINE

### EXTERIOR

| | |
|---|---|
| **WALLS** | Stucco and wood siding |
| **ROOF** | Heavy wood shingles |
| **WINDOWS** | Wood, double hung |
| **COLOR** | Walls, trim and doors— white<br>Roof—natural<br>Blinds—green |

### INTERIOR

| | |
|---|---|
| **FLOORS** | Living rooms, bed- rooms and halls—oak<br>Kitchen—linoleum<br>Baths—tile |
| **WALLS** | Living rooms and halls —plaster, painted<br>Bedrooms—wallpaper<br>Kitchen—Sanitas<br>Baths—tile and wall- paper |
| **CEILINGS** | Plaster, painted. Baths —Sanitas, painted |
| **LIGHTING** | Direct. Bright brass fix- tures |
| **CUBAGE** | 26,400 cubic feet |

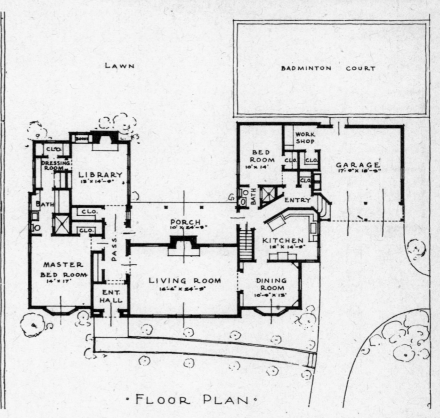

· FLOOR PLAN ·

When planning your entrance hall, consider the advantages of a table for mail, cards and packages, of a chair for pulling on rub- bers and for laying a hat and coat when not bothering with the coat closet, and of a mirror. Special provision must be made for this furniture; otherwise it may be discovered too late that the four walls have been completely filled by doors, windows and stairs. This small hall adapts itself to such furnishings.

The close connection established here between the library and bedroom, and its separation from the living room, suggests an in- timate use, partaking of the character of an upstairs sitting room in a two-story house. This suite, with its own approach to the rear lawn, permits the living room to be treated formally, and to be reserved for entertaining.

A porch situated like this one may be used in mild climates as a supplementary passage between the bedroom wing and the service quarters. Notice how the garage roof has been given a wide over- hang to provide a sheltered way from the service entrance. This treatment also makes the garage doors less conspicuous. The work- shop is adequate in size, is well lighted, and has a closet for locking up equipment.

HERTZKA AND KNOWLES, ARCHITECTS

FIRST FLOOR

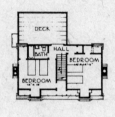

SECOND FLOOR

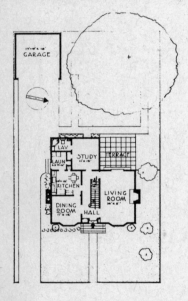

Several practical items are illustrated by this house. The letter slot by the front door is connected to a metal box built into the wall, which supplies a safe place for receiving the mail. The circle in the kitchen closet represents a revolving ant-proof cooler, where food that does not require the low temperature of a refrigerator may be kept. Vents create a circulation of air, while a special construction keeps away ants.

The first-floor laundry combined with a service porch is included in most California homes, whether or not they have cellars. There are so many points in its favor that it seems necessary to mention only a few. The danger and nuisance of dark steep cellar stairs is eliminated, the tubs are near the clothesline, and washing and ironing are less of a chore, for they may be fitted in better with the regular household duties. The laundry should include two wash tubs, a collapsible drying rack, an ironing board that folds into the wall, and a closet for laundry supplies. Space should also be provided for a washing machine and electric ironer, as well as the clothes basket. With a service porch the outside door may be left unlocked when expecting deliveries, locking the kitchen door instead.

## DESCRIPTIVE OUTLINE

### EXTERIOR

| | |
|---|---|
| WALLS | Stucco |
| ROOF | Cedar shingles |
| WINDOWS | Wood, double hung |
| COLOR | Walls, trim and doors— egg-shell white<br>Roof—natural |

### INTERIOR

| | |
|---|---|
| FLOORS | Living rooms, bed-rooms and halls—oak<br>Kitchen—linoleum<br>Baths—tile |
| WALLS | Living rooms and kitchen—plaster<br>Study, bedrooms and halls—wallpaper<br>Baths—tile wainscot |
| CEILINGS | Plaster |
| LIGHTING | Direct |
| CUBAGE | 24,129 cubic feet. House, 20,024; garage, 4,105 |

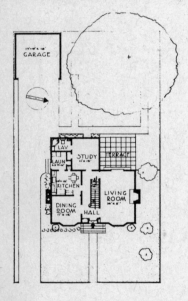

ALLEN G. SIPLE, ARCHITECT

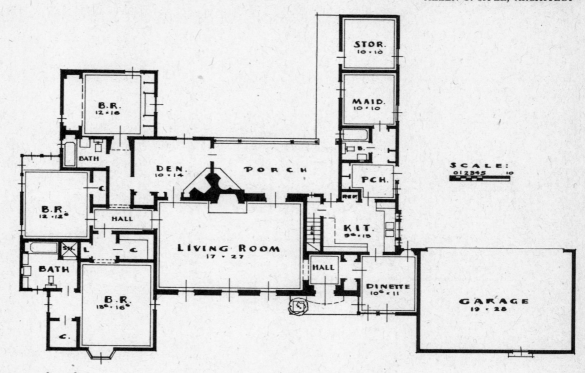

## DESCRIPTIVE OUTLINE

### EXTERIOR

| | |
|---|---|
| WALLS | Brick veneer and redwood siding |
| ROOF | Cedar shingles |
| WINDOWS | Steel casement |
| COLOR | Walls—white<br>Roof—natural<br>Sash aluminum<br>Blinds—olive green |

### INTERIOR

| | |
|---|---|
| FLOORS | Living rooms, bedrooms and halls—oak<br>Baths—tile and linoleum |
| WALLS | Wallpaper and painted canvas |
| CEILINGS | Painted |

The owner of this house wished a small estate with the character of a farm which would serve as relaxation from his busy life in the city. The problem, then, was to incorporate the benefits of modern planning and equipment into a building of long rambling lines suitable for a country site. This length has been gained partially by the judicious use of the three-car garage, which extends the building thirty feet, yet seems a part of it owing to the continuation of the main roof. The service wing likewise seems long, but this is due somewhat to the store room, useful but not necessarily costly feature.

The plan is quite compact for a one-story house with such ample accommodations. The entrance hall is small, yet contains two closets and space for a table, mirror and chair. The dinette is of minimum size, but the corner window and concentration of doors allow sufficient room for furniture designed in small scale. Meals may also be served on the sheltered porch, where the fireplace will take off the chill of a cool day. The location of the den permits it to be easily converted into a bedroom.

Kitchen shown on page 59.

EDGAR BISSANTZ, ARCHITECT
ROMA COOLIDGE MULVIHILL, LANDSCAPE ARCHITECT

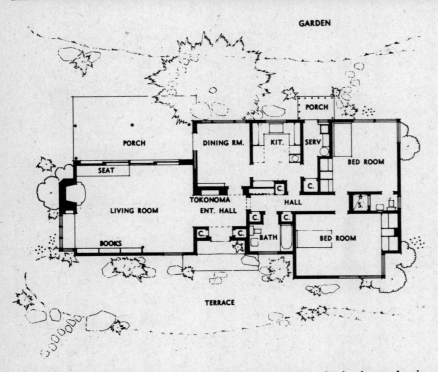

The owner of this house wished to incorporate in it the esthetic appeal of the Orient without sacrificing the advantages of contemporary American planning. Thus, although the Oriental influence is evident in the finesse of the design, in the delightful landscaping treatment and in a detail or two, no attempt has been made to borrow heavily from its architecture.

The plan is particularly straightforward and practical. All rooms are grouped about a central hall so that none are used as passages. Their position has been determined by the beautiful mountain scenery to the rear. The windows, which are generous in area, are also governed by this view and by the arrangement of furniture.

The tokonoma is the place of honor in a Japanese house. It consists of a platform several inches above the floor in a simply treated alcove. On the wall behind is hung a valuable painting or calligraph below which is placed a vase of flowers. Both picture and vase are changed frequently, great care being spent each time to obtain a lovely composition. Even without its ceremonial significance the beauty of the tokonoma would be a welcome addition to the decoration of to-day's home.

Entrance detail shown on page 21. Living room shown on page 51.

## DESCRIPTIVE OUTLINE

### EXTERIOR

| | |
|---|---|
| WALLS | Cement plaster |
| ROOF | Cedar shingles |
| WINDOWS | Wood casement |
| COLOR | Walls—light grey-green<br>Roof—natural<br>Trim — burnt-rose, chartreuse and grey |

### INTERIOR

| | |
|---|---|
| FLOORS | Living rooms, bedrooms and halls—1"x6" Douglas fir, oiled<br>Kitchen, baths and service porch—linoleum |
| WALLS | Living room, bedrooms and halls—smooth, sand-finished plaster oiled a light warm grey color<br>Dining room—Japanese grass cloth<br>Kitchen and baths—Sanitas and enamel |
| CEILINGS | Living room—ivory finished Celotex with small wood battens<br>Elsewhere—plaster |
| CUBAGE | 19,930 cubic feet |

H. ROY KELLEY, ARCHITECT

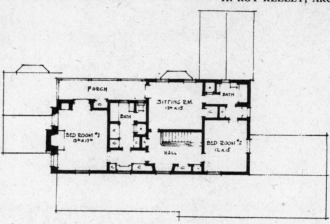

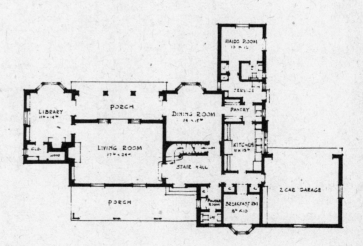

## DESCRIPTIVE OUTLINE

### EXTERIOR

| | |
|---|---|
| WALLS | Adobe brick veneer and wide pine siding |
| ROOF | Wood shingles |
| WINDOWS | Wood, double hung |
| COLOR | Walls—white<br>Roof—reddish-brown<br>Blinds—green |

### INTERIOR

| | |
|---|---|
| FLOORS | Living rooms, bedrooms and halls—oak<br>Kitchen—linoleum<br>Owner's bath—rubber tile<br>Other baths—tile |
| WALLS | Living room and halls—plaster, painted<br>Library—pine boarding, stained light and waxed<br>Dining room and bedrooms—wallpaper |
| CEILINGS | Plaster, painted |
| CUBAGE | 52,824 cubic feet |

The repetition of the decisive horizontal lines of the main roof in that of the entrance porch and again in the roof of the breakfast room and garage extension ties this house firmly to its site. The stair hall supplies a direct approach to the living room, dining room, cellar stairs, kitchen, garage, breakfast room and powder room, a notable achievement in planning. A powder room is a convenience for guests and family alike, but does not occupy much space. It contains a dressing table with useful drawers, and serves not only as a coat closet, but also as a vestibule for the lavatory beyond. It may also be used as a telephone room. It is desirable that both powder room and lavatory have a window. The large closet off the library includes a smaller closet and a wood box. The upstairs sitting room may be easily converted into a bedroom, for it has a closet and connecting bath, and is not depended upon for passage to another room.

87

ROLAND E. COATE, ARCHITECT

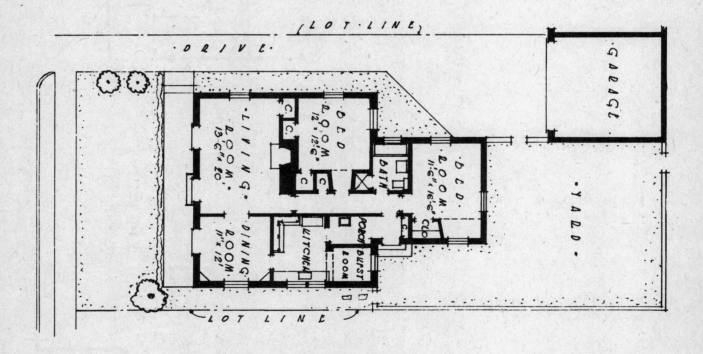

An interesting point to be noted here is how an idea used on a large house can be adapted to a much smaller one. On account of differences in scale, however, such transposition of motifs is not always successful, and must be done cautiously, for a treatment suitable for one might be overpowering on the other, and vice versa. The brick terrace extending the width of this elevation is similar to that of the house by the same architect shown on page 77. It has been reduced in scale to accord with the design of this house, but its value in furnishing a broad solid setting for the architecture is still apparent. The French doors supply an additional reason for its inclusion here. The lot is extremely narrow, and yet the building does not look compressed.

The service entrance acts as a yard or garden door likewise. It is not necessary to pass thru the kitchen when going to the yard; from the bedroom hall it takes just a couple of steps across the narrow service porch to get outdoors.

## DESCRIPTIVE OUTLINE
### EXTERIOR

| | |
|---|---|
| WALLS | Brick veneer |
| ROOF | Shakes |
| WINDOWS | Wood casement |
| COLOR | Walls, trim and doors —white |
| | Roof—natural |
| | Blinds—dark |

HERTZKA AND KNOWLES, ARCHITECTS

## DESCRIPTIVE OUTLINE

### EXTERIOR

| | |
|---|---|
| WALLS | Stucco and redwood boards with battens |
| ROOF | Hand-split cedar shingles |
| WINDOWS | Wood, double hung |
| COLOR | Walls, trim and doors —light cream<br>Roof—natural<br>Blinds—green |

### INTERIOR

| | |
|---|---|
| FLOORS | Living room and dining room—random oak plank<br>Study, bedrooms and hall—oak<br>Kitchen—linoleum<br>Baths—tile |
| WALLS | Living room, dining rooms, bedrooms, hall —stucco<br>Study—knotty pine<br>Kitchen—plaster<br>Baths—tile wainscot |
| CEILINGS | Living room, dining room, bedrooms and hall—stucco<br>Study—exposed beams<br>Kitchen and baths— plaster |
| LIGHTING | Direct |
| CUBAGE | 21,929 cubic feet |

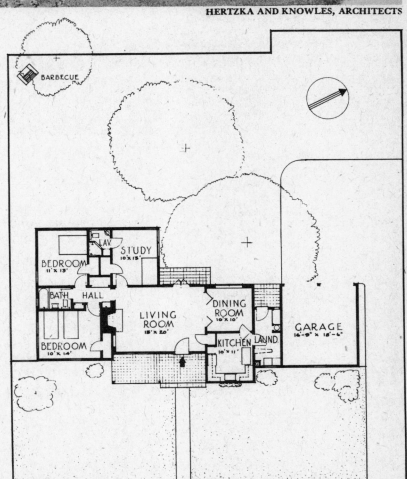

This plan provides the conveniences desired in a small house in a straightforward manner without a waste of space. The living room has a coat closet, built-in bookshelves, and a door to the rear yard. Around a minimum-size hall are grouped the bedrooms, with cross-ventilation, a bath, and closets for linen, brooms and storage. The study with its own bath is a flexible room, adaptable as a sitting room, guest room, or regular bedroom, accommodating changes in the size of the family. The dining room is small, but it can open out into the living room by folding back the doors that form one wall. It is easy to work in the kitchen. Range, sink, refrigerator, closet and counters are within a step of each other, and still off the line of passage through the room. Against the inside wall is a place for a table and chairs. The first-floor laundry and attached garage complete the layout.

H. ROY KELLEY, ARCHITECT

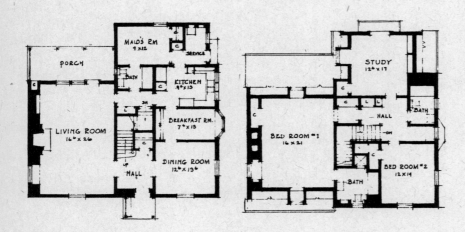

The difference in grade of a front lawn may be taken up in a steep bank, leaving the rest of the area level. Steps are then required. They are a hazard, particularly in the dark, but warning of them may be given by a gate, as done here.

The position of street numbers is often a last-minute consideration, and so they are generally hard to read, particularly at night. They have played an important role in the design of this doorway. The numerals are large, the wall behind them smooth although all other wall surfaces are rough, and the light is admirably located.

The house faces the street, but the living room extends through to the rear, supplying direct access to the porch overlooking the garden. The breakfast room is fitted with a counter for facilitating serving, and with cupboards above for storage. The maid's room is entered from the service porch, but her bath has a door to the passage from the living room; this permits its use as a first-floor lavatory. The extra linen closet opposite this door is a convenience.

## DESCRIPTIVE OUTLINE

### EXTERIOR

| | |
|---|---|
| WALLS | Stone and split cedar shakes |
| ROOF | Cedar shingles |
| WINDOWS | Wood, double hung and casement |
| COLOR | Stone walls—white Shakes—grey-white Roof—warm brown Blinds—white |

### INTERIOR

| | |
|---|---|
| FLOORS | Living rooms, bedrooms and halls—oak Kitchen and baths—linoleum |
| WALLS | Living room, dining room, breakfast room and bedrooms—wallpaper |
| CEILINGS | Painted |
| CUBAGE | 33,720 cubic feet |

R. M. SCHINDLER, ARCHITECT

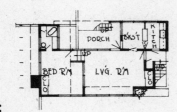

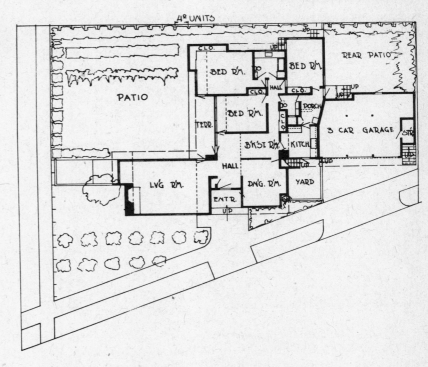

# DESCRIPTIVE OUTLINE

## EXTERIOR

| | |
|---|---|
| WALLS | Stucco |
| ROOF | Composition |
| WINDOWS | Sliding sash of sheet metal, cadmium plated. Sliding screens |
| COLOR | Walls—white<br>Roof—white<br>Doors—aluminum |

## INTERIOR

| | |
|---|---|
| FLOORS | Living rooms and bedrooms—carpet<br>Halls and kitchen—linoleum<br>Baths—tile |
| WALLS | Living rooms, bedrooms and halls—interior stucco<br>Kitchen and baths—Sanitas |
| CEILINGS | Living rooms, bedrooms and halls—interior stucco<br>Kitchen and baths—Sanitas |
| LIGHTING | Concealed |

This is really a one-story residence with a small but complete apartment for a relative cleverly located over the garage. Such an arrangement not only eliminates the expenses incidental to owning and maintaining two entirely separate establishments, but assures accommodations close at hand. Communication is maintained here by the stairs leading down from the upper porch to the rear patio. However, the apartment has its own street entrance to the right of the garage. Thus each household may be run individually, and each group may lead its own life.

In connection with the owner's quarters, a rear patio has been included as a protected play space for children. The front patio is then reserved for the older members, and the lawn and shrubs do not become damaged. The plan is capable of an unusual openness, for the large glass areas are sliding metal sashes. The projection of horizontal planes above the windows keeps out excessive sunlight. All closets are equipped with sliding doors.

Entrance facade shown on page 11.

WILLIAM WILSON WURSTER, ARCHITECT

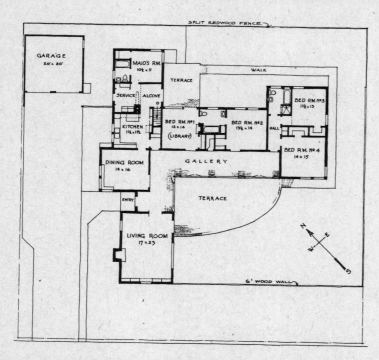

This plan is distinguished by the way an asset has been made of the conventional hall. The whole house is built about the gallery, which in turn opens out pleasantly to the terrace and lawn. Although such a use of glass would add a feeling of breadth to even a simple corridor, this gallery has been liberally proportioned, becoming a spacious sunroom, besides providing easy and cheerful circulation among the rooms. To enhance the value of this treatment, the house has been set well back on the lot, leaving plenty of space on the south front. The living room, together with the six foot wall, screens the gallery and terrace from both the street and the adjoining houses.

The drawback to this arrangement is that the desirable exposure of the gallery is sometimes gained at a sacrifice of the outlook from other rooms. Here that fact has been recognized by the inclusion of a supplementary terrace on the rear with a walk connecting the two areas. The drive and entrance have been carefully kept apart from the outdoor living quarters. The double width of the drive permits several cars to be parked on it at one time without blocking it.

Gallery shown on page 63.

## DESCRIPTIVE OUTLINE

### EXTERIOR

| | |
|---|---|
| WALLS | Flush redwood siding |
| ROOF | Cedar shingles |
| WINDOWS | Wood, double hung, casement and fixed frames |
| COLOR | Walls—yellow<br>Roof—natural<br>Trim and doors—yellow and brown-grey |

### INTERIOR

| | |
|---|---|
| FLOORS | Living rooms and bedrooms—oak<br>Gallery, terraces and entry—brick<br>Kitchen, service and baths—linoleum |
| WALLS | Gallery—flush redwood siding<br>Library, kitchen and alcove—pine wall board<br>Elsewhere—plaster |
| CEILINGS | Kitchen and alcove—wood<br>Elsewhere—plaster |
| LIGHTING | A minimum of fixtures. Mostly by table lamps |
| CUBAGE | 3,268 square feet or approximately 35,000 cubic feet |

SPENCER AND LANDON, ARCHITECTS

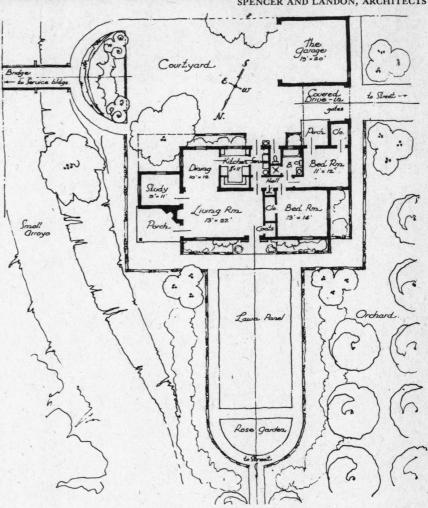

## DESCRIPTIVE OUTLINE

### EXTERIOR

**WALLS** — Grout lock brick masonry

**ROOF** — Cedar shingles

**WINDOWS** — Steel casement

**COLOR** — Walls—off-white with grey-blue dado
Roof—natural
Trim, blinds and doors —off-white

### INTERIOR

**FLOORS** — Living rooms, bedrooms and hall—oak
Kitchen—linoleum
Bath—tile

**WALLS** — Living rooms, bedrooms and hall—exposed brick masonry
Kitchen and bath— Sanitas

**CEILINGS** — Living rooms, bedrooms and halls—exposed wood framing
Kitchen and bath— Sanitas

**LIGHTING** — Direct

**AREA** — 1,636 square feet

This unaffected elevation illustrates how charm may be imparted to a building by good proportion, careful arrangement of windows, simple low-pitched roofs and judicious landscaping. If these basic elements are satisfactorily worked out, decoration of any kind is not only superfluous, but very likely harmful. The character of the design has rightly been influenced by the French descent of the owners. The lawn panel helps the facade with a suitable setting.

Under ordinary circumstances exception might be taken to the circuitous connection between the courtyard and the front door. Entrance through a service porch or bedroom is not always pleasant for the owner, and certainly never attractive for guests. The plan itself is exceedingly well integrated and efficient. The plumbing is concentrated to eliminate extra piping, a minimum length of hall is required, and the openness between living and dining rooms and the elimination of an entrance hall develop to the utmost the limited floor area available.

HARWELL HAMILTON HARRIS, DESIGNER

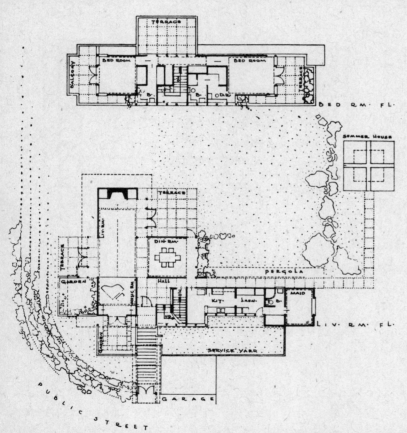

## DESCRIPTIVE OUTLINE

### EXTERIOR

| | |
|---|---|
| WALLS | 12″ vertical boards with battens, stained |
| ROOF | Redwood shingles |
| WINDOWS | Wood casements |
| COLOR | Walls—brown<br>Roof—aluminum<br>Doors—ochre |

### INTERIOR

| | |
|---|---|
| FLOORS | Dining room, music room, second floor hall, bedrooms and part of living room—carpet<br>First floor hall and parts of living room next to the terraces—flagging<br>Kitchen and baths—linoleum |
| WALLS | Living rooms and halls—redwood<br>Bedrooms—white pine plywood<br>Kitchen and baths—enamel |
| CEILINGS | Living rooms, bedrooms and halls—Celotex<br>Kitchen and baths—enamel |
| LIGHTING | Direct and semi-indirect. Mostly built-in |
| CUBAGE | 21,000 cubic feet plus garage, basement and terraces |

There is no attempt made to follow any stylistic precedent with this house. Rather the walls, windows and roof are designed to enhance the utility of the interior arrangement and to realize to the fullest the magnificent views from the hilltop site. Although the plan is basically similar to other contemporary ones in providing for both a separation of household activities and a good circulation between rooms, it is distinguished by its openness and mergence with the outdoors. A minimum of partitions defines the dining and music rooms. The dotted squares represent flagging that is carried into the living room and hall to connect the inside with the gardens. A similar expansion of room sizes is accomplished by the French doors opening from the music room and bedrooms to individual terraces with high wood walls for privacy and protection from the winds. The high-silled windows on the second floor are appropriate for the baths and dressing room, precluding the necessity for shades.

H. ROY KELLEY, ARCHITECT

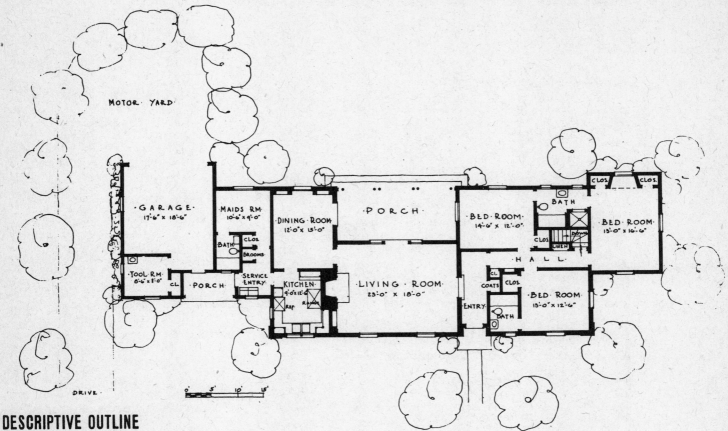

## DESCRIPTIVE OUTLINE

### EXTERIOR

| | |
|---|---|
| WALLS | Brick veneer and cement plaster |
| ROOF | Wood shingles |
| WINDOWS | Wood, double hung and casement |
| COLOR | Walls, trim and blinds —light buff<br>Roof—medium brown |

### INTERIOR

| | |
|---|---|
| FLOORS | Living rooms, bedrooms and baths—oak<br>Kitchen—linoleum<br>Baths—tile |
| WALLS | Plaster, painted |
| CEILINGS | Plaster, painted |

This type of plan, with the living room separating the bedrooms from the service quarters, is very apt to produce such a building of charm and long restful lines as this house. Since its longer dimension is usually parallel with the street, it presents a more imposing facade than a square plan of the same accommodations, but it quite obviously demands a wider lot. By providing an effective isolation for the service quarters it overcomes the objection to the one-story house that living rooms, bedrooms and kitchen are figuratively all on top of one another. This is an important point where a maid is employed, but in a servantless household this advantage must be weighed against the extra steps required to do the housework. A living room with windows on the two long walls is easy to furnish, for furniture groups can be arranged on both sides of the room, and still receive plenty of natural light. Here, on the other hand, the entire length of the room has to act as a passage between the parts of the house, which not only disturbs the privacy, but necessitates that a wide path be left from end to end for easy circulation.

96

CURTIS CHAMBERS, ARCHITECT

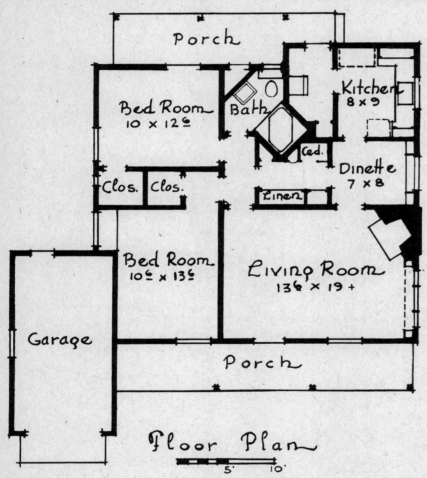

Floor Plan

This utterly simple and pleasing elevation manages to include a garage that extends toward the street and yet does not become obtrusive. This is in part due to the low eaves line and the broad expanse of the gently-pitched roof, which gives unity to the design. The rooms are so arranged that very little hall space is required. To preserve the comfort and quiet of a living room, it is better to provide communication from the entrance door to the various rooms by halls than to employ the living room as a traffic artery. Yet this often results in long circuitous corridors, which are cheerless in themselves, and limit the possibilities of the plan. With the open planning of to-day this refinement is frequently sacrificed for a greater spaciousness. With central heat, rooms no longer need be shut off to conserve the warmth of an open fire-or to prevent cold drafts. The prime consideration in using the living room for circulation, however, is the matter of cost. Considerable cubage is saved, a vital factor with the small house, where expense is important.

## DESCRIPTIVE OUTLINE

### EXTERIOR

| | |
|---|---|
| WALLS | Stucco |
| ROOF | Cedar shingles |
| WINDOWS | Wood casement |
| COLOR | Walls—white Roof—tobacco brown Blinds—yellow |

### INTERIOR

| | |
|---|---|
| FLOORS | Living rooms, bedrooms and hall—oak Kitchen and bath—linoleum |
| WALLS | Living room and dinette—pine Elsewhere—light buff interior stucco |
| CEILINGS | Light buff interior stucco |
| CUBAGE | 15,000 cubic feet |

**SPENCER AND LANDON, ARCHITECTS**

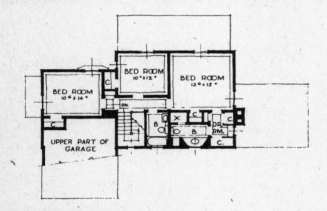

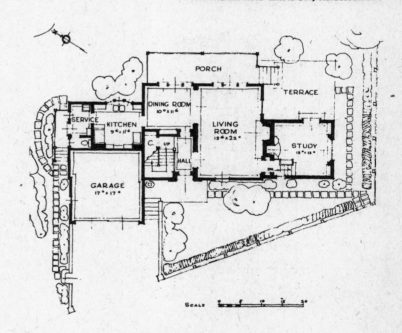

## DESCRIPTIVE OUTLINE

### EXTERIOR

| | |
|---|---|
| WALLS | Grout lock brick masonry, stucco and cedar siding |
| ROOF | Wood shingles |
| WINDOWS | Steel casement |
| COLOR | Walls—off-white and weathered siding Roof—natural Trim, blinds and doors —off-white |

### INTERIOR

| | |
|---|---|
| FLOORS | Living rooms, bedrooms and halls—oak Kitchen—linoleum Baths—tile |
| CEILINGS | Living room—exposed beams Elsewhere—plaster |
| LIGHTING | Direct |
| AREA | 2,204 square feet |

The plan for a hillside house must not only be good in itself; it must fit the location in question. To do so it must be carefully considered in relation to the grades, and a proper level established for the first floor. Factors to take into account are a setting for the building, and a flat area, even though small, for a garden or terrace, so that you are not confined to the indoors. This house has been definitely worked out for its site. The garage is at the street level for ease in backing out. The entrance is below the road to keep the building as close as possible to the ground. The level front yard provides a feeling of stability, while the excavated earth is used as a fill for the terrace in the rear. The study is down five steps more, so that easy access may be had from it to this terrace. The plan opens out toward the extensive view. Every room has at least one window on the rear, but the house presents almost a blank wall toward the street.

HERTZKA AND KNOWLES, ARCHITECTS

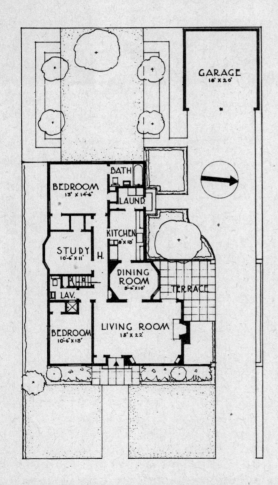

It is hard to realize that there are six rooms behind this pleasant little elevation. In spite of the narrow lot, however, space is found for a terrace with direct access from the living room, providing also an outlook from the dining room bay window. Its privacy is assured by a brick wall, but advantage is taken of every inch of the width of the property by including the drive in this court.

A recessed entrance not only gives a sheltered doorway but supplies a place for a coat closet adjacent to the door, a most convenient spot. Here the slight alcove created on the other side suggests a separation of the door from the living room. When the front door leads directly into the living room, a piece of furniture may be used to give the semblance of a hall without sacrificing the size of the room. A screen is particularly effective, for it may also be employed to keep drafts from the places where people sit.

## DESCRIPTIVE OUTLINE

### EXTERIOR

| | |
|---|---|
| WALLS | Stucco |
| ROOF | Cedar shingles |
| WINDOWS | Wood, double hung |
| COLOR | Walls, trim, blinds and doors—egg-shell white Roof—white |

### INTERIOR

| | |
|---|---|
| FLOORS | Living rooms, bedrooms and halls—oak Kitchen—linoleum Baths—tile |
| WALLS | Living room—wood wainscot and plaster Study—wallpaper Dining room, bedrooms, halls and kitchen—plaster Baths—tile wainscot |
| CEILINGS | Plaster |
| LIGHTING | Direct |
| CUBAGE | 21,050 cubic feet House 17,250. Garage 3,800 |

MARSTON AND MAYBURY, ARCHITECTS

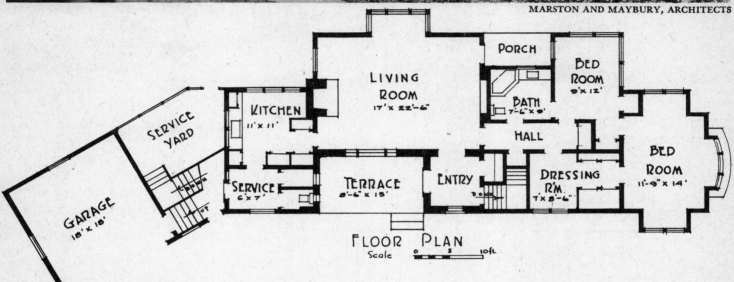

FLOOR PLAN
Scale 0 5 10ft.

## DESCRIPTIVE OUTLINE
### EXTERIOR

| | |
|---|---|
| WALLS | Brick veneer, wood siding and wood shingles |
| ROOF | Cedar shingles |
| WINDOWS | Wood, double hung |
| COLOR | Walls—old white<br>Roof—natural<br>Trim and doors—white<br>Blinds—green |

### INTERIOR

| | |
|---|---|
| FLOORS | Living rooms, bedrooms and halls—oak<br>Kitchen and baths—linoleum |
| WALLS | Living rooms, bedrooms and halls—wallpaper<br>Kitchen and baths—painted |
| CEILINGS | Living rooms, bedrooms and halls—fine sand-finished plaster<br>Kitchen and baths—painted |

Because it presents its full length to the street, this house appears quite sizeable. Likewise, the plan looks comfortable and ample, but upon further examination it is realized that the building is really not large but extended. The floor area has been intensively developed, leaving no waste space. Though the entry and dressing room could be dispensed with if the requirements had to be reduced to a minimum, they add appreciably to the enjoyment of the house.

The expense of a separate lavatory, located on the first floor of a two-story house, may be saved with a one-story type. This bath is convenient for the bedrooms, but is also near the living room and entry.

The value of a bedroom for anything besides sleeping is often seriously impaired by failure to consider, when planning, the location of the beds. Consequently they project into the room, cutting the floor into small worthless areas. Here a single bed will fit into each of the two alcoves with the high windows in the master bedroom, leaving the rest of the room unusually open with plenty of space for lounging. The large bay window at the end is thus particularly effective.

Entrance detail shown on page 8

DONALD D. MCMURRAY, ARCHITECT

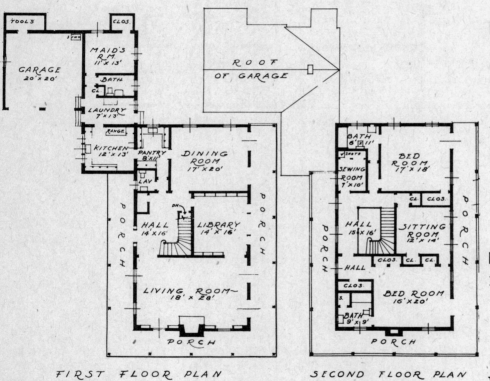

FIRST FLOOR PLAN          SECOND FLOOR PLAN

## DESCRIPTIVE OUTLINE

### EXTERIOR

| | |
|---|---|
| WALLS | Stucco |
| ROOF | Shingle tile |
| WINDOWS | Wood, double hung |
| COLOR | Walls and porches—light buff<br>Roof—dark brown to black<br>Trim, sash and doors—bottled green |

### INTERIOR

| | |
|---|---|
| FLOORS | Living rooms—oak plank<br>Bedrooms and halls—oak<br>Kitchen—linoleum<br>Baths—tile |
| WALLS | Living rooms, bed-rooms and halls—interior stucco<br>Kitchen — Sanitas, enameled<br>Baths—tile and Sanitas, enameled |
| CEILINGS | Living rooms, bed-rooms and halls—interior stucco<br>Kitchen and baths—Sanitas, enameled |
| LIGHTING | Direct. Wrought iron fixtures |
| AREA | 3,500 square feet |

Covered porches for each floor are typical of buildings in the tropics, where protection from both a hot sun and heavy rains is necessary. Such a treatment may also be appropriately employed for houses in milder climates and for summer places. The porches are not intended for outdoor living, and so are not wide. They rather extend a friendly feeling, and develop a delightful airiness. French doors allow you to escape from the feeling of confinement imposed by the walls of a room. From a practical standpoint the shelter afforded the windows permits them to be left open when it rains, so that the interior is kept from becoming hot and close. The porches appreciably increase the size of the building, preventing the street elevation here from looking thin. Yet the slender posts and delicate railings do not efface the body of the house.

The principal rooms overlook a side lawn, but this house has its entrance on the opposite side, preserving a seclusion for the garden. The drive with its broad gateway defines the approach, while the close relationship established between the drive, entrance and garage is convenient.

WILLIAM WILSON WURSTER, ARCHITECT

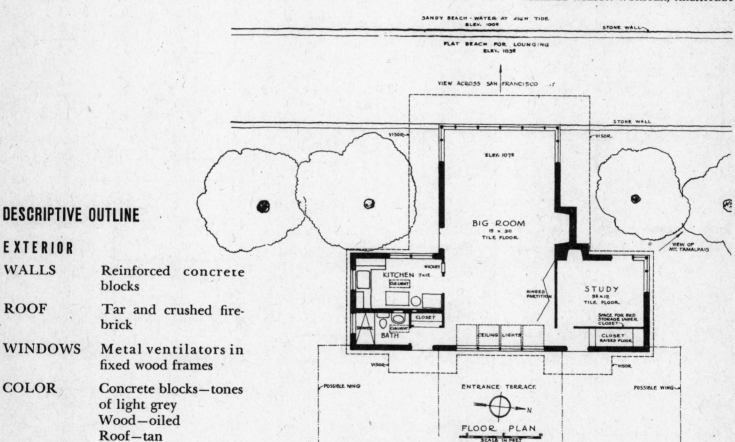

SANDY BEACH · WATER AT HIGH TIDE.
ELEV. 100±

STONE WALL

FLAT BEACH FOR LOUNGING
ELEV. 103±

VIEW ACROSS SAN FRANCISCO ...y

STONE WALL

VISOR

VISOR

ELEV. 107±

BIG ROOM
15 x 30
TILE FLOOR.

VIEW OF MT. TAMALPAIS

WICKET

KITCHEN 7x12

CLG.LIGHT

CLOSET

HINGED
PARTITION

STUDY
9x12
TILE FLOOR.

SPACE FOR BED
STORAGE UNDER
CLOSET

SHOWER

CLG.LIGHT

BATH

CEILING LIGHTS

CLOSET
RAISED FLOOR

VISOR

VISOR

POSSIBLE WING

ENTRANCE TERRACE.

POSSIBLE WING

N

FLOOR PLAN
SCALE IN FEET

## DESCRIPTIVE OUTLINE

### EXTERIOR

**WALLS** — Reinforced concrete blocks

**ROOF** — Tar and crushed fire-brick

**WINDOWS** — Metal ventilators in fixed wood frames

**COLOR** — Concrete blocks—tones of light grey
Wood—oiled
Roof—tan

### INTERIOR

**FLOORS** — 12″ x 12″ hollow tile

**WALLS** — Exposed concrete blocks. Plywood partitions, untreated

**CEILINGS** — Celotex

**LIGHTING** — Flush ceiling l i g h t s. Table lamps

**CUBAGE** — 816 square feet or approximately 7,800 cubic feet

The week-end house serves as a retreat from the city. It differs from the summer cottage in that the latter offers the accommodations of a complete home in a plain and limited fashion, whereas the former attempts little more than to provide a place for eating and sleeping with effortless housekeeping. The plan should be informal and compact, with adequate storage space provided for sporting equipment. Notice that the floor of the large closet is raised so that an extra cot can be stored under it. Privacy and flexibility of space, here supplied by the study and the hinged partition respectively, are two other desirable items. Large windows and easy access to the outdoors permit the fullest enjoyment of Nature. This house has taken on the character of a boat by being placed near the water's edge. The view from within shows only water and the mountains across the Bay, for the beach in the foreground is cut off by the window sill.

ALLEN G. SIPLE, ARCHITECT

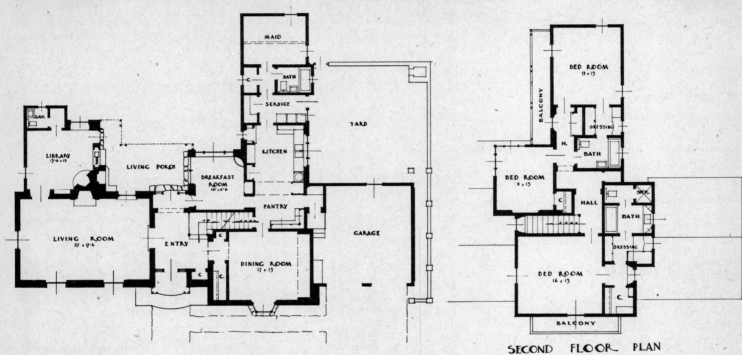

FIRST FLOOR PLAN

SECOND FLOOR PLAN

This house has more generous accommodations than the facade indicates. From the street it appears primarily as a one-story building with the long horizontal line of the cornice tying it to the ground. Since the house is set several feet above the street level, it might seem unpleasantly high if it presented a full two-story wall on the front. With the garage near the street, and the service centered about a neat walled yard, the whole rear of the lot is left free for lawn and gardens. The built-in incinerator in one corner of the yard is a useful thing.

The second floor has been thoughtfully arranged. All bedrooms have cross ventilation, yet the beds need not be in a draft. At times wall space in a bedroom is spoiled, or the floor becomes a mere passage, simply by a careless disposition of doors. Here they have been limited to two for each room, and these are near each other. A dressing room offers the most satisfactory method of providing for clothes, and need not be extravagant of space.
Entrance detail shown on page 23.

## DESCRIPTIVE OUTLINE

### EXTERIOR

| | |
|---|---|
| WALLS | Stucco and redwood vertical boarding |
| ROOF | Cedar shingles |
| WINDOWS | Wood casement |
| COLOR | Walls and trim—white Roof—grey |

### INTERIOR

| | |
|---|---|
| FLOORS | Living rooms, bedrooms and halls—oak Baths—tile and linoleum |
| WALLS | Wallpaper and painted canvas |
| CEILINGS | Painted |

MARSTON AND MAYBURY, ARCHITECTS

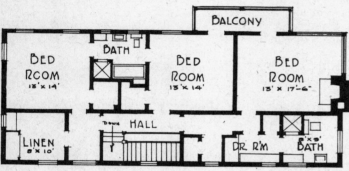

SECOND FLOOR PLAN

## DESCRIPTIVE OUTLINE

### EXTERIOR

| | |
|---|---|
| WALLS | Stucco |
| ROOF | Wood shingles |
| WINDOWS | Wood, double hung |
| COLOR | Walls—cream<br>Roof—natural<br>Trim and doors—white<br>Blinds—green |

### INTERIOR

| | |
|---|---|
| FLOORS | Living rooms, bedrooms and halls—oak<br>Kitchen and service porch—linoleum<br>Baths—tile |
| WALLS | Living rooms, bedrooms and halls—interior stucco<br>Kitchen, service porch and baths—smooth plaster, painted |
| CEILINGS | Living rooms, bedrooms and halls—interior stucco<br>Kitchen, service porch and baths—smooth plaster, painted |

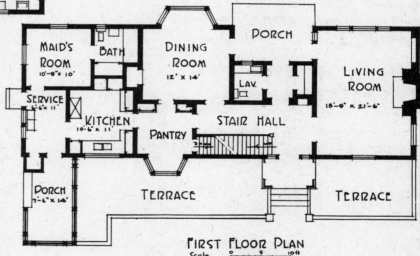

FIRST FLOOR PLAN
Scale

One factor that determines the plan of a house is the outlook. Few sites can offer such magnificent mountain scenery as shown here. More likely the view is limited to a lawn and garden, artificially created in conjunction with the house. Even so, the same approach is followed in the design. This plan reserves the view at the rear for the important rooms, placing service and halls toward the street.

The doors to the porch from the living and dining rooms are placed on the side walls, leaving the ends of the rooms for the wide windows. These doors, with the one from the hall, make the porch readily accessible. The second floor balcony, besides providing more shelter for the porch below, permits French doors in the bedrooms. These are protected from rain by the roof of the balcony. French doors admit plenty of fresh air, and give the feeling of being outside, the advantages of a sleeping porch. In addition, they present a view of the landscape while lying in bed; through the ordinary window not much more than the sky is visible.

EDGAR BISSANTZ, ARCHITECT

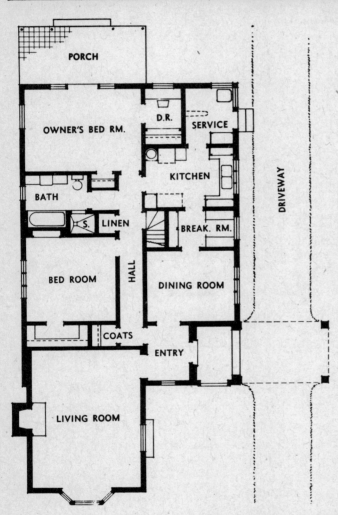

This house possesses a freshness and individuality seldom found in the small city residence. The entrance is at the side, but is well marked by both the porte-cochere and the lattice of the porch. Circulation is provided by the hall, so that it is not necessary to use any room as a passage to another. The probable location of furniture was also carefully considered, resulting in long, unbroken wall surfaces. By enlarging a closet and adding a window, a simple dressing room may be developed like the one off the owner's bedroom here. One side is equipped with a pole for clothes-hangers and a shelf for hats and boxes; the other with a dressing table and drawers under the window. The blank wall between supplies a place for a full-length mirror. The problem of the architect was to design an economical house for a narrow lot, and he pleasantly achieves it.

## DESCRIPTIVE OUTLINE

### EXTERIOR

| | |
|---|---|
| WALLS | Cement plaster |
| ROOF | Cedar shingles |
| WINDOWS | Wood, double hung |
| COLOR | Walls—very pale green with olive green base<br>Roof—natural<br>Trim—white |

### INTERIOR

| | |
|---|---|
| FLOORS | Living rooms, bedrooms and halls—oak<br>Kitchen, breakfast room and service porch—linoleum<br>Bath—tile |
| WALLS | Living room and hall—plaster<br>Dining room and bedrooms—wallpaper<br>Kitchen, breakfast room and service porch—Sanitas and enamel |
| CEILINGS | Living room—wood<br>Elsewhere—plaster |
| LIGHTING | Direct. Polished brass Colonial fixtures except for chromium plated ones in service rooms |
| CUBAGE | 22,100 cubic feet |

RICHARD J. NEUTRA, ARCHITECT    PETER PFISTERER, COLLABORATOR

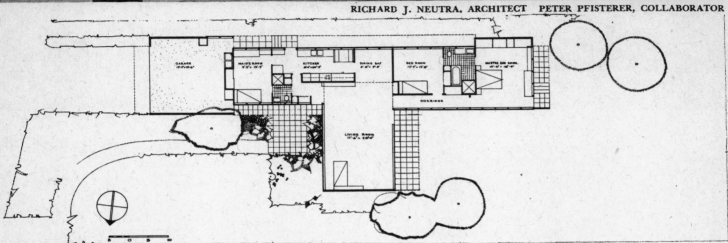

## DESCRIPTIVE OUTLINE

### EXTERIOR

| | |
|---|---|
| WALLS | Cement p l a s t e r and sheet-steel |
| ROOF | Composition |
| WINDOWS | Steel; fixed, casement and projected |
| COLOR | Cement plaster—oyster shell<br>Sheet-steel, s a s h and wood—aluminum |

### INTERIOR

| | |
|---|---|
| FLOORS | Living rooms, bed-rooms and hall—carpet<br>Kitchen—linoleum |
| WALLS | L i v i n g room—¼" plate glass, S a n i t a s painted and Philippine mahogany<br>Master bedroom and h a l l—Sanitas painted and Philippine mahogany<br>Kitchen—tile and San-itas painted<br>Elsewhere—S a n i t a s, painted |
| LIGHTING | Indirect, controlled by rheostat |

This house is an extremely successful solution for a narrow lot. It also embodies architectural principles for their intrinsic value alone, and attempts no picturesque revival of the horse-and-buggy days. The garage is near the street for several reasons. The expense of a long drive is reduced, backing is minimized, the house is shielded somewhat from street noises, and the rear yard is left free for landscaping. In a cold climate there would be little snow to remove to keep the drive open. Behind the garage is the service. The kitchen is an efficient, almost inconspicuous workroom adjacent to the front door, and does not occupy the whole rear of the house as it would have formerly. Next comes the large living room, with windows on the front to take advantage of mountain scenery, and windows on the rear to overlook the outdoor living area. At the very back, where it is the quietest, are the bedrooms.

Notice the hood over the garage door, the covered walks from the garage to the front and service doors, and the rows of windows, especially in kitchen and baths. Still the house has a comfortable character and is not a mere machine for living.

Living room shown on page 61. Dining alcove shown on page 55.

WILLIAM WILSON WURSTER, ARCHITECT

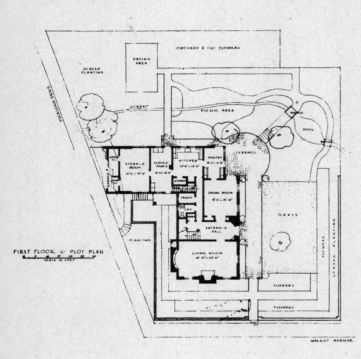

FIRST FLOOR OF PLOT PLAN

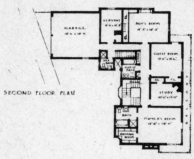

SECOND FLOOR PLAN

## DESCRIPTIVE OUTLINE
### EXTERIOR

| | |
|---|---|
| WALLS | Brick veneer and cement plaster |
| ROOF | Cedar shingles |
| WINDOWS | Wood, double hung except steel casements to balcony |
| COLOR | Walls and trim—linen color<br>Roof—natural<br>Soffit of eaves—sky-blue |

### INTERIOR

| | |
|---|---|
| FLOORS | Living rooms, bedrooms and halls—oak<br>Kitchen—linoleum<br>Baths—tile |
| WALLS | Library and boy's room—redwood<br>Elsewhere—plaster |
| CEILINGS | Living room—wood<br>Elsewhere—plaster |
| LIGHTING | A minimum of fixtures. Indirect in dining room. Mostly by table lamps |
| CUBAGE | 3,828 square feet or approximately 41,000 cubic feet |

Sun, view, or the shape of a lot may suggest that the principal rooms of a house look out over a side yard, and that the terrace and gardens be located there also. To accomplish this a plan with its greater dimension at right angles to the street is likely to be most satisfactory. So that the hall may be centrally located, the entrance will probably be placed on one of the long sides. It is often possible to choose whether to put it on the garden side or on the opposite one. With this house, however, it was necessary to choose the garden side, so that the doorway would be easy to find. The only approach to this house is from below, for the road ends shortly beyond the garage. When the entrance is on the garden side, the outdoor living area loses some privacy. On the other hand, an attractive path and friendly welcome are provided, while the outside is readily accessible from all the rooms by way of the hall. The circular terrace in this foreground is spared the traffic to the front door, and is close to the pantry for serving.

CURTIS CHAMBERS, ARCHITECT

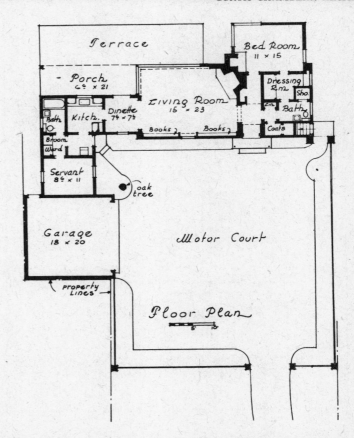

## DESCRIPTIVE OUTLINE

### EXTERIOR

| | |
|---|---|
| WALLS | Stucco |
| ROOF | Cedar shingles |
| WINDOWS | Steel casement |
| COLOR | Walls—cream<br>Roof—natural<br>Trim—white with<br>maroon accents<br>Blinds and doors—<br>white |

### INTERIOR

| | |
|---|---|
| FLOORS | Living rooms, bed-rooms and hall—broad-loom carpet<br>Kitchen—linoleum<br>Baths—tile |
| WALLS | Light buff interior stucco |
| CEILINGS | Living rooms, bed-rooms and halls—light buff interior stucco<br>Kitchen and baths—painted |
| LIGHTING | Direct and indirect |
| CUBAGE | 17,500 cubic feet |

With a motor court the nuisance of a blocked drive is obviated, there is ample turning area, and a fitting location is provided for the garage doors. Since the house is designed in relation to it, parked cars seem a part of the picture, whereas, when left on a drive, they tend to disturb the setting. Here the long, low facade and the motor court with the bold rail fence combine to impart the character of a country estate to this small house of a bachelor.

The plan, influenced by the fine oak and the view of the mountains to the east, is also determined by the fact that the site is bordered on the south by a fire station and on the north by a service station. To offset this the house is placed well to the rear of the lot, about 175 feet from the street. The garage hides the service station, while only the dressing room and bath suffer from the fire station.

Entrance hall with coat closet, dressing room, open and covered terraces, and servant's quarters are refinements not often found in such limited space.

WINFIELD SCOTT WELLINGTON, ARCHITECT

## DESCRIPTIVE OUTLINE

### EXTERIOR

| | |
|---|---|
| WALLS | Resawn redwood boards and battens treated with boiled linseed oil |
| ROOF | Cedar shingles |
| WINDOWS | Wood casement |
| COLOR | Walls—dark reddish brown<br>Roof—grey<br>Soffit of eaves and sash—blue-green |
| FLOORS | 1" x 4" Oregon pine stained a dark green-brown |
| WALLS | Kitchen—wallboard, enameled<br>Elsewhere—frame of 3" x 4" Oregon pine studs, 30" on centers, and wide sheathing boards left exposed and stained a soft French green |

### INTERIOR

| | |
|---|---|
| CEILINGS | Exposed framing, stained a soft French green<br>Kitchen—wallboard enameled |
| LIGHTING | Chinese goathorn lanterns hung from ceilings of living room and hall. Convenience outlets |
| CUBAGE | 17,512 cubic feet |

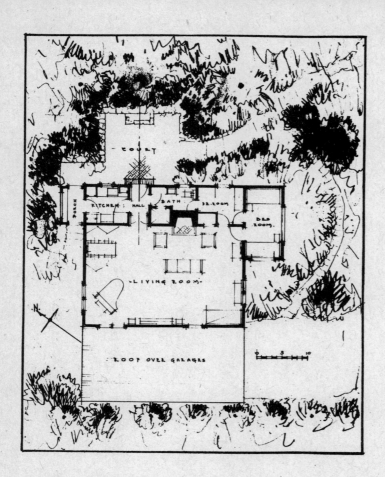

This plan combines the ease of operation of a week-end house with a more formal mode of life than is usual in such restricted quarters. The living room, its ceiling extending to the rafters, is large enough to contain a grand piano without crowding, but is not used for sleeping. The efficiently arranged and well ventilated bedroom with its connecting dressing room and bath provides a desirable separation in a compact manner. The kitchen is small, but entirely workable; the open porch increases its serviceability, and provides a useful built-in seat.

The refinements of the plan are continued on the exterior; the brick-paved court presents a pleasant approach, desirable in such a thickly-grown countryside. The parallel slopes of the roofs harmonize with the hillside, and the garage fits in well on the lower level. However, for most situations the plan would be improved by the substitution of a deck off the living room for the sloping roof of the garage.

MARSTON AND MAYBURY, ARCHITECTS

FIRST FLOOR PLAN

LIVING
ROOM
19'-6" X 30'-6"

LIBRARY
15'X16'

STAIR
HALL
15'-4" X 19'

DINING
ROOM
16' X 19'

PORCH
10'-8" X 17'

PORCH

COVERED TERRACE
10'-6" X 30'

PANTRY
9'X 10'

KITCHEN
15'X 14'

SERVICE

TOOLS

GARAGE
21'-6" X 30'

SECOND FLOOR PLAN

MASTER
BED
ROOM
19' X 20'

DR. RM.

BATH

BED
ROOM
12'-8" X 19'

BATH

DR. RM.

GUEST
ROOM
14'-8" X 15'-4"

MAID'S
ROOM
11' X 13'-10"

PORCH

BALCONY
9'-6" X 29'-4"

## DESCRIPTIVE OUTLINE

### EXTERIOR

WALLS — Brick veneer, stucco and vertical redwood boarding

ROOF — Heavy shakes

WINDOWS — Wood, double hung

COLOR — Walls—very pale green
Roof—natural
Trim and doors—white
Blinds—dark green

### INTERIOR

FLOORS — Living rooms and halls—oak plank
Bedrooms—oak
Kitchen and s e r v i c e porch—linoleum
Baths—rubber tile

WALLS — Living rooms, bedrooms and halls—wallpaper and interior stucco, slightly troweled
Kitchen and b a t h s—Sanitas, painted

CEILINGS — Plaster, fine sand finish

The views are particularly splendid from three sides of this site. Consequently a long, narrow plan with a projecting wing for the living room has been required. Four rooms are then given the unusual feature of triple exposure, so the large, covered terrace at the entrance and another off the living room do not darken them. The square, walled porches on the corner have architectural importance in preventing the library wing from appearing too thin, as well as in terminating the horizontal lines of the balcony. From a practical standpoint they shelter the terrace from that angle. The upper one may be used as a sleeping porch. The stair hall presents a delightful vista across the living room and through the large bay window at the end to the mountains beyond. The library, dining room, coat closet, lavatory and service portion open neatly from this hall also.

Entrance detail shown on page 25.

ARTHUR L. HERBERGER, ARCHITECT

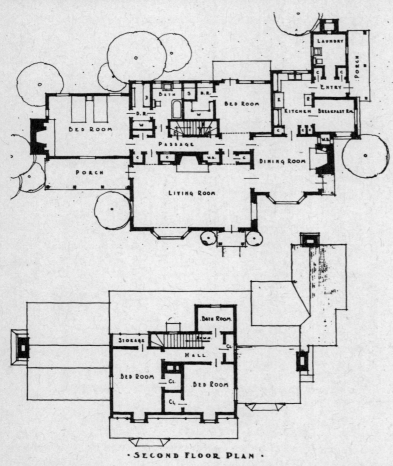

· SECOND FLOOR PLAN ·

This is a good example of how a house may appear to have a traditional character, and impart the charm of a Colonial cottage, and yet reflect contemporary living customs. The massive chimneys, copied from models at Williamsburg, and the dormer windows belong to houses of yesterday, but the generous bay windows and the liveable plan date the house as of today. Close contact with the grounds is maintained by the doors from living room to porch, from the small bedroom to its own terrace, and from the dining room. The principal bedrooms are on the first floor, where they can enjoy a full ceiling height and ample windows, and where their closets or dressing rooms can be satisfactorily equipped, and not be cut into by the slope of the roof, a disadvantage of the story-and-a-half house.

Service porch shown on page 35.

## DESCRIPTIVE OUTLINE

### EXTERIOR

| | |
|---|---|
| WALLS | 1″ x 10″ beveled redwood siding |
| ROOF | Cedar shingles |
| WINDOWS | Wood, double hung |
| COLOR | Walls, trim and doors —off-white<br>Roof—natural<br>Blinds—green |

### INTERIOR

| | |
|---|---|
| FLOORS | Dining room—random oak plank<br>Living room and bedrooms—oak<br>Kitchen—linoleum<br>Baths—tile |
| WALLS | Dining room—white pine boards<br>Living room and bedrooms—wallpaper<br>Kitchen and baths—Sanitas |
| CEILINGS | Living room and dining room—wood<br>Bedrooms and halls—plaster<br>Kitchen and baths—Sanitas |
| LIGHTING | Direct |
| CUBAGE | 20,000 cubic feet |

H. ROY KELLEY, ARCHITECT

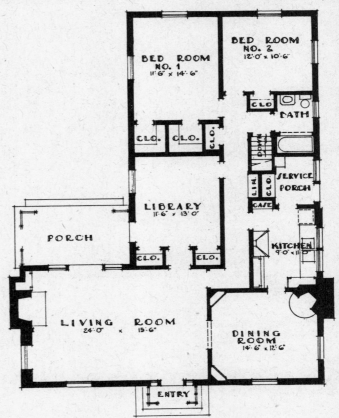

## DESCRIPTIVE OUTLINE

### EXTERIOR

| | |
|---|---|
| WALLS | Beveled wood siding |
| ROOF | Wood shingles |
| WINDOWS | Wood, d o u b l e hung and casement |
| COLOR | Walls, trim and doors—white<br>Roof—medium brown<br>Blinds—blue-green |

### INTERIOR

| | |
|---|---|
| FLOORS | Living rooms, bedrooms and hall—oak<br>Kitchen—linoleum<br>Bath—tile |
| WALLS | Living room—vertical pine b o a r d i n g and wallpaper<br>Dining room and bedrooms—wallpaper<br>Elsewhere—p l a s t e r, painted |
| CEILINGS | Plaster, painted |

The street elevation of this house has one window on each side of a center door, a treatment similar to that of the house shown on page 98. It is interesting to compare the minor variations of two plans when the requirements are practically identical. The problem in each case was to design a six-room, one-story house for a narrow lot, with a terrace or porch immediately accessible from the living room. The floor areas are nearly equal, one house having slightly larger rooms, while the other has a second bath.

In both examples the kitchen may be entered from the hall. An effective separation of the service group is not thus obtained, and cooking odors and noises can the more readily spread through the house. On the other hand, a great many steps are saved, and household duties are lightened. For example, preparing breakfast may be fitted in with dressing. Where a maid is not employed, a too rigid division of activities is not always advisable.

Living room shown on page 48.

WILLIAM WILSON WURSTER, HALL AND PROETZ, ASSOCIATED ARCHITECTS

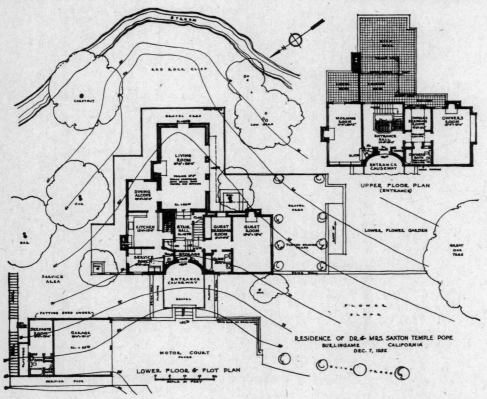

UPPER FLOOR PLAN
(ENTRANCE)

RESIDENCE OF DR. & MRS. SAXTON TEMPLE POPE
BURLINGAME    CALIFORNIA
DEC. 7, 1932

LOWER FLOOR & PLOT PLAN

## DESCRIPTIVE OUTLINE

### EXTERIOR

| | |
|---|---|
| WALLS | Brick veneer and flush redwood siding |
| ROOF | Tar and gravel. Slate deck |
| WINDOWS | Steel projected. Steel French doors in living room |
| COLOR | White except for lead-colored leaders |

### INTERIOR

| | |
|---|---|
| FLOORS | Living rooms, bedrooms and halls—oak Kitchen and baths—linoleum |
| WALLS | Living room—brick, painted Elsewhere—plaster |
| CEILINGS | Plaster |
| LIGHTING | A minimum of fixtures. Mostly by table lamps |
| CUBAGE | 3,383 square feet or approximately 36,000 cubic feet |

A site so precipitous might discourage many, but the close connection here between the contours and the building has produced a house of distinction. It opens out on the sunny side of the valley to terraced gardens and a vista up the stream. The projection of the living room takes advantage of a point of land formed by a bend in the stream. The narrow terrace around this wing gives communication on the exterior, and also suggests that the house has a firm base.

The drive is cut out of the hillside, but there is room for a paved motor court where the grade flattens out. The wide causeway, softened by planting strips on each side, leads to the entrance hall, which is on the upper floor. Off this are the owner's suite and a large deck, partly roofed, which makes a fine sleeping porch. By itself on a level six steps lower is a quiet morning room or library. The main stair descends around an open well to a landing from which the guest-room is entered, then continues down to the high-ceiled living room.

KENNETH S. WING, ARCHITECT

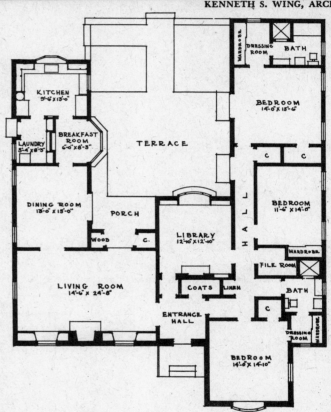

## DESCRIPTIVE OUTLINE

### INTERIOR

WALLS      Brick veneer and cement plaster. Vertical boarding at living room porch

ROOF      Cedar shingles

WINDOWS      Wood, double hung

COLOR      Walls, trim, blinds and doors—off-white
Roof—natural

### EXTERIOR

FLOORS      Entry—parquetry
Library—oak plank
Living room, dining room, bedrooms and halls—oak
Breakfast room, kitchen and service porch—linoleum
Baths—tile

WALLS      Library—wood, stained
Living room—one wall wood, enameled; others—wallpaper
Kitchen—Sanitas
Baths—tile wainscot and Sanitas

CEILINGS      Plaster, painted

LIGHTING      Direct

CUBAGE      36,000 cubic feet

The breakfast room may seem a waste of space. However, its good points should be considered before planning your home. The furnishings are easy to use and keep clean: linoleum floor, simple furniture and an unpretentious table setting. Consequently, meals are served here more readily than in a dining room, while the convenience of eating in the kitchen is afforded without the disagreeableness of doing so. It is suitable for breakfast, lunch and maid's-night-out suppers. It is also fine for children's meals, besides making an indoor play space that can be supervised from the kitchen. In conjunction with the modern kitchen, which is sometimes so compact that there is no room for a table, it provides a place where the maid can sit down to her meals. Furthermore, it may be located to benefit by the morning sun, while the dining room may be given a western exposure.

Although a position between kitchen and dining room may appear to lengthen needlessly the distance between the two, the breakfast room then, in addition to the above advantages, forms a vestibule that keeps cooking odors from the rest of the house. Also, it can act as a serving pantry for the dining room.

GARDNER A. DAILEY, ARCHITECT

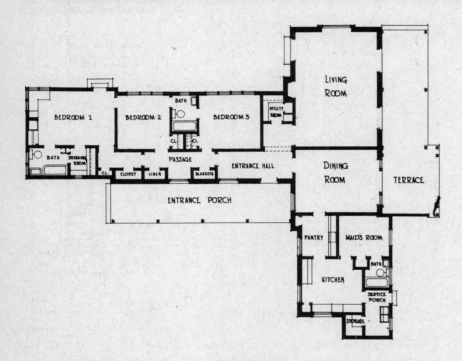

A slight difference in grade allows the edge of this motor court to be defined by a low retaining wall, separating it from the grounds about the house. The circular brick platform in the corner serves to call attention to the walks. The porch on the front commands a view of mountains to the west, while the sunny terrace off the living room overlooks a valley. With two outdoor living areas on opposite sides of the house, one may be used when it is too windy or warm to sit on the other.

Owing to improved methods of building and heating, and the diminished need for storage facilities, the full cellar has become a waste of space and money, even in cold climates. It can sometimes be eliminated completely, and a small heater-room substituted on the first floor. This house is warmed by individual gas heaters in the floor, two in the halls and one in the kitchen. However, the large coat closet behind the living room fireplace suggests a location for a furnace where central heat is necessary.

Terrace shown on page 33. Owner's bedroom shown on page 69.

## DESCRIPTIVE OUTLINE

### EXTERIOR

| | |
|---|---|
| WALLS | Brick veneer and red-wood siding |
| ROOF | Redwood shingles |
| WINDOWS | Wood casement |
| COLOR | Walls, trim, blinds and doors—white<br>Roof—brown |

### INTERIOR

| | |
|---|---|
| FLOORS | Living rooms, bedrooms and halls—oak<br>Owner's bedroom—carpet<br>Kitchen and baths—linoleum<br>Service porch—concrete |
| WALLS | Plaster |
| CEILINGS | Plaster |
| LIGHTING | Flush ceiling boxes and table lamps |
| CUBAGE | 28,800 cubic feet |

SPENCER AND LANDON, ARCHITECTS

SECOND FLOOR PLAN

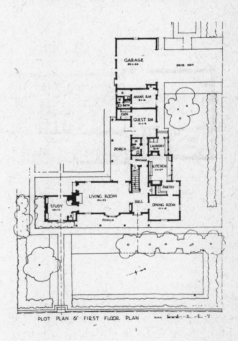

PLOT PLAN & FIRST FLOOR PLAN

## DESCRIPTIVE OUTLINE

### EXTERIOR

WALLS — Stucco and wood siding

ROOF — Wood shingles

WINDOWS — Wood, double hung

COLOR — Walls, trim and doors
—off-white
Roof—natural
Blinds—green

### INTERIOR

FLOORS — Living rooms, bedrooms and halls—carpented oak
Kitchen—linoleum
Baths—tile

WALLS — Living rooms, bedrooms and halls—wallpaper
Kitchen and baths—Sanitas and tile

CEILINGS — Plaster

LIGHTING — Direct

AREA — 3,498 square feet

This L-shaped plan fully develops the advantages of a corner lot. An imposing elevation is presented on the front, while the kitchen and laundry enjoy an abundance of light and air from the side street, and need not overlook the garden. Thus the large, comfortable porch has a southern exposure and is centrally located, but does not deprive any room of its only light source. The garage requires only a short drive. Backing out is easier and safer into the side street, where traffic is lighter, than into the roadway in front. The disadvantage of a corner lot is its loss of privacy for outdoor living. This has been overcome here by using the service wing as a screen.

Both visitors and family appreciate a guest room separated from the other bedrooms. The guest feels freer, for he is not obliged to take such a close part in the routine of the household. The man's room and the maid's room are prudently placed at a distance from each other, even though it does require an extra bath.

WILLIAM WILSON WURSTER, ARCHITECT

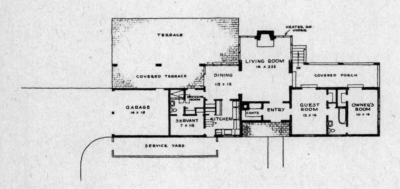

## DESCRIPTIVE OUTLINE

### EXTERIOR

| | |
|---|---|
| WALLS | Resawn beveled redwood siding |
| ROOF | Cedar shingles |
| WINDOWS | Wood, double hung and fixed frames |
| COLOR | Walls and trim—light blue<br>Roof—natural |

### INTERIOR

| | |
|---|---|
| FLOORS | Living rooms, bedrooms and baths—Douglas fir<br>Kitchen—linoleum |
| WALLS | White pine boards and white pine plywood |
| CEILINGS | White pine boards and white pine plywood |
| LIGHTING | A minimum of fixtures. Mostly by table lamps |
| CUBAGE | 1,817 square feet or approximately 19,500 cubic feet |

A house on a hill may have a splendid outlook and no suitable place outside from which to enjoy it. This house, obviously designed to capitalize the commanding views, overcomes this disadvantage. Its relation to the contours of the land allows room for a comfortable paved terrace. Planting beds are concentrated here to be fully enjoyed, while the rest of the property is in its natural state. This treatment might well be used for the country house where the rough land is not conducive to landscaping, or where it is desired to minimize the upkeep of the grounds and still give a cultivated look to the outdoor living area.

The simple, low-pitched roof, extending from end to end unbroken save for the living room projection, and including the porches under its smooth surfaces, contributes much to the restfulness of the building. The covered porch leading to the owner's bedroom might be glazed to keep out the weather, decorated with objects on shelves against the windows, and so converted into a sunny gallery. The service entrance on the street front is hidden by a wooden fence that forms a small service yard.

Living room shown on page 62.

CHARLES O. MATCHAM, ARCHITECT

## DESCRIPTIVE OUTLINE

### EXTERIOR

**WALLS** Hollow cement building tile reinforced by solid concrete studs. Exterior finish—stone tile, painted

**ROOF** Shingle tile

**WINDOWS** Steel casement

**COLOR** Walls—white with green dado
Roof, trim and blinds —green

### INTERIOR

**FLOORS** Living rooms and screened porch—cement
Bedrooms and halls— hardwood
Kitchen and baths—linoleum

**WALLS** Living rooms and halls —exposed stone tile
Bedrooms and baths— wallpaper
Kitchen—enamel

**CEILINGS** Living room—exposed wood roof framing
Bedrooms and halls— plaster
Kitchen and baths— enamel

**CUBAGE** 32,000 cubic feet

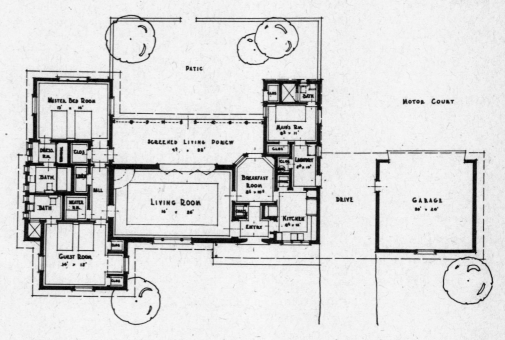

When placed directly against a house, the attached garage is likely to cover a great deal of the valuable exterior wall surface, besides requiring a circuitous path from street to service entrance. Laying the drive between house and garage overcomes both of these disadvantages. Then, by means of a roof over the drive integral with that of the garage, the wing again becomes incorporated into the body of the house. What is more, the building appears larger and more impressive, and its proportions very likely have been improved at slight additional expense (except that a wider lot is necessary). At the same time, a sheltered connection between house and garage is maintained.

This dressing room is a simple, practical arrangement: a wardrobe on one side and a dressing table on the other. With the bath adjacent not many steps need be taken in the course of dressing. Both here and in the baths two narrow windows have been installed instead of the customary larger single one. Thus, when one looks in a mirror over the dressing table or the lavatories, both sides of the face are evenly lighted.

Entrance detail shown on page 21.

H. ROY KELLEY, ARCHITECT

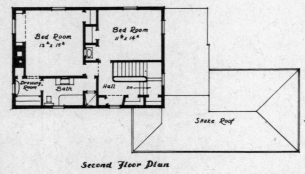

Second Floor Plan

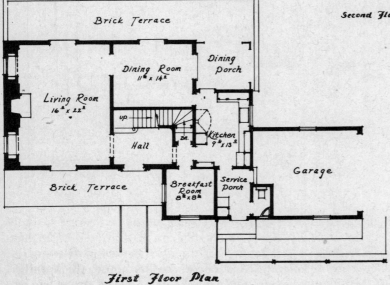

First Floor Plan

## DESCRIPTIVE OUTLINE

### EXTERIOR

| | |
|---|---|
| WALLS | Cement plaster |
| ROOF | Cedar shingles |
| WINDOWS | Wood casement |
| COLOR | Walls, trim and blinds —warm white<br>Roof—natural<br>Entrance door—blue-green |

### INTERIOR

| | |
|---|---|
| FLOORS | Living rooms, bed-rooms and halls—oak<br>Kitchen and baths—linoleum |
| WALLS | Living room—smooth plaster, painted<br>Dining room—wall-paper<br>Elsewhere—plaster, painted in warm white tones |
| CEILINGS | Plaster, painted. Living room a delphinium blue |

The rear elevation of this simple and pleasing house is shown here. A firmness is suggested by the horizontal lines of the long brick terrace, while a note of gaiety is imparted by the espalier treatment of the wall. The dining porch on the left is ideally located with reference to kitchen, dining room and garden. Meals may also be conveniently served beyond the terrace at the table under the umbrella.

The plan is extremely workable and efficient, without being in the least bit cramped. The cheerful halls are of an appropriate size and are not long corridors. The breakfast room may also be used as a study, or even as a maid's room. A wall hides the service entrance from the street. The lavatory in a closet off the smaller bedroom relieves the burden on the one bathroom.

Entrance detail shown on page 24. Stair shown on page 66.

HERVEY PARKE CLARK, ARCHITECT
THOMAS D. CHURCH, LANDSCAPE ARCHITECT

## DESCRIPTIVE OUTLINE

### EXTERIOR

WALLS    1″x10″ resawn redwood boards laid flush

ROOF    Cedar shingles

WINDOWS    Wood casement

COLOR    Walls and trim—off-white
Roof—natural
Entrance door—lacquer red

### INTERIOR

FLOORS    Living rooms, bedrooms and halls—hardwood
Kitchen, pantry and baths—linoleum

WALLS    Plaster. Dining room—natural colored burlap hung loosely

CEILINGS    Living room—1″x8″ resawn redwood boards laid flush
Elsewhere—plaster

LIGHTING    Dining room—concealed in soffit

CUBAGE    49,789 cubic feet

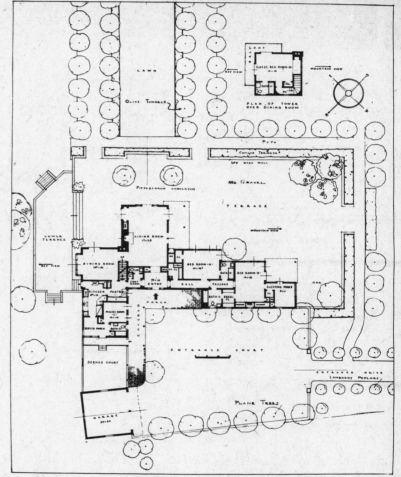

Owing to the commanding situation of this house, the specific problem in its design was to give each room a view of either bay or mountains, and direct access to an outdoor living terrace or balcony. The entrance court leads to the entry, which has been skilfully developed as a junction for the three elements of the house. The living quarters are ahead, the bedroom wing to the right, and the service wing to the left. The guest room has privacy and a splendid location in the tower over the dining room. Closets are plentiful, several of them being included for specific purposes, like the utility closet for slop sink, pressing, linen and winter clothing, a specially ventilated closet for outing clothes and fishing tackle, a store room for terrace furniture, a closet for painting and drawing materials, and a wood box beside the living room fireplace.

The terrace is surfaced with red gravel, thus eliminating the care of a grass lawn.

Living room shown on page 47.

ARTHUR R. HUTCHASON, ARCHITECT
TOMMY TOMSON, CONSULTING LANDSCAPE ARCHITECT

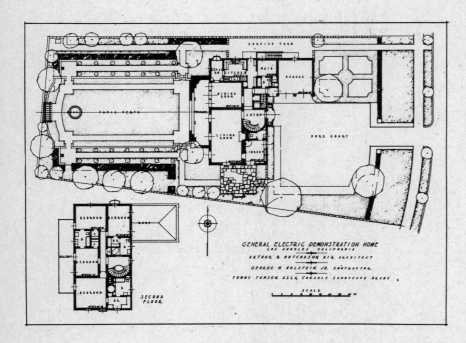

## DESCRIPTIVE OUTLINE

### EXTERIOR

| | |
|---|---|
| WALLS | Stucco |
| ROOF | Wood shingles |
| WINDOWS | Wood casement |
| COLOR | Walls, trim, blinds, doors—off-white Roof—natural |

### INTERIOR

| | |
|---|---|
| FLOORS | Living rooms and halls —parquetry Bedrooms—carpet Breakfast room and kitchen—linoleum Baths—rubber tile |
| WALLS | Living room—Sanitas, painted Library, dining room and breakfast room— wallpaper above wainscot Bedrooms—wallpaper Kitchen—tile Baths—glass and wallpaper |
| CEILINGS | Sanitas, painted |
| LIGHTING | Direct. Brass, silver and crystal fixtures |
| CUBAGE | 47,900 cubic feet |

This lot is relatively small for such a large house, but the landscaping plan has developed the available land to the utmost, obtaining the effect of a larger plot. This has been accomplished by the concentration of areas with similar functions, and a consequent elimination of unrelated pieces. For example, the space usually taken by a drive and front lawn has been used for a forecourt, certainly a more practical arrangement, and here just as effective for setting off the house. Likewise, the entire rear yard has been devoted to one garden, with the center grass area or tapis verte unifying the scheme as well as providing a foreground for the garden elevation. The remaining strips on the north and south sides have been entirely given over to a service yard and an open terrace respectively, both screened by brick walls.

Both plans and elevations provide for a rather formal living standard. At the same time liveableness has been a prime consideration in the disposition of the rooms. Unbroken wall surfaces for beds and a concentration of doors make the bedrooms easy to furnish.

ROLAND E. COATE, ARCHITECT
KATHERINE BASHFORD, LANDSCAPE ARCHITECT

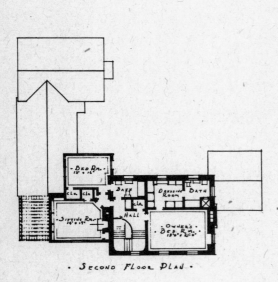

· SECOND FLOOR PLAN ·

· FIRST FLOOR PLAN ·

There is an interesting relation between the dominating and rather severe stone body of this house, set off by the center lawn panel on both front and rear, and the more informal porch and service wing of rough shakes.

The first floor living quarters are spacious and uncomplicated, containing only the wide hall, the living room, almost square, and the dining room. The large porch is convenient to the living room, but does not darken it. Its corner location gives it an exposure on all four sides, yet it does not seem loosely attached to the building. Blinds for its openings give privacy and shade at will without obstructing air circulation.

The second floor is devoted principally to the owner's comfort. Stair hall, master bedroom, dressing room and sitting room are so large that the guest room seems small in comparison. It can be combined with the sitting room and bath to create a pleasant suite. Entrance detail shown on page 24.

## DESCRIPTIVE OUTLINE

### EXTERIOR

| | |
|---|---|
| WALLS | Stone and shakes |
| ROOF | Shakes |
| WINDOWS | Wood, double hung |
| COLOR | Walls, trim, blinds and doors—white<br>Roof—natural |

MARSTON AND MAYBURY, ARCHITECTS

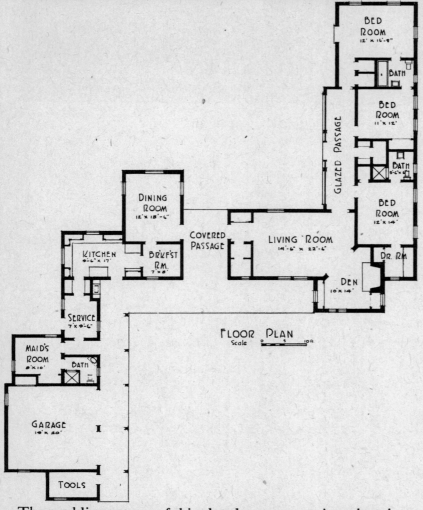

FLOOR PLAN
Scale 0 5 10 ft.

The rambling pattern of this plan deserves attention where heating is not a problem. The service wing and garage on the left define a spacious forecourt; the bedroom wing partly encloses a garden, easily reached from all rooms.

An unusual feature about the house is the unpretentious, covered passage which has been substituted for the ordinary entrance hall. This is reminiscent of the breezeway in Southern homes, which is a path cut through a building to create a circulation of air on hot days. It develops an openness impossible with the conventional hall. The wide Dutch doors serve as entrance doors, and allow the house to be closed. Where protection must be provided against cold weather, this mergence with the outdoors may be achieved in part by filling the two ends with glazed doors and fixed sashes.

The glazed passage leading to the bedrooms is more cheerful than a corridor, and helps to connect house and garden. Its slight extra width and broad glass areas make of it a sun room, a pleasant addition at little expense.

## DESCRIPTIVE OUTLINE

### EXTERIOR

| | |
|---|---|
| WALLS | Brick veneer, vertical boarding and cement plaster |
| ROOF | Cedar shingles |
| WINDOWS | Wood, double hung and casement |
| COLOR | Walls, trim and doors—oyster white<br>Roof—natural<br>Blinds—oak green |

### INTERIOR

| | |
|---|---|
| FLOORS | Parquetry laid in mastic on concrete slab. |
| WALLS | Living rooms, bedrooms and halls—interior stucco, troweled smooth<br>Kitchen and baths—painted |
| CEILINGS | Living rooms, bedrooms and halls—interior stucco, troweled smooth.<br>Kitchen and baths—painted |

KENNETH S. WING, ARCHITECT

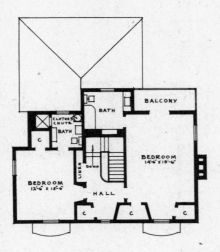

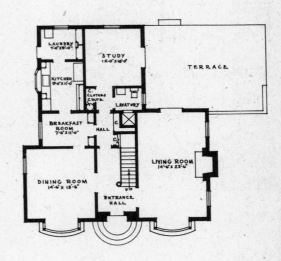

## DESCRIPTIVE OUTLINE

### EXTERIOR

| | |
|---|---|
| WALLS | Cement plaster |
| ROOF | Cedar shingles |
| WINDOWS | Wood, double hung |
| COLOR | Walls and trim—off-white<br>Roof—black<br>Blinds—blue-green |

### INTERIOR

| | |
|---|---|
| FLOORS | Oak |
| WALLS | Living rooms, bedrooms and halls—wallpaper<br>Kitchen—Sanitas |
| CEILINGS | Painted |
| LIGHTING | Direct. Flush ceiling boxes in dining room, breakfast room and kitchen |
| CUBAGE | 34,000 cubic feet |

Although this house appears like the traditional two-story Colonial model with a center stair hall, close examination discloses refinements unknown to our forefathers and a thoughtful adaptation to present-day living. To begin with, the entrance door is recessed two feet to provide shelter. The broad bay windows on each side of it admit quantities of sunshine to the dining and living rooms. The latter opens directly upon a rear terrace. The study, which may be easily converted into a bedroom, shares this terrace, but also serves as a buffer to the service quarters. An extra depth has been added to the cupboards off the rear hall for the storage of card tables.

The second floor likewise expresses to-day's mode of living. The bedrooms, each with its own bath, are generous in size, and have plenty of closet space. The covered balcony off the owner's room allows the use of French doors for easy access to the open air. The metal-lined clothes chute is one step toward simplifying the laundry problem.

H. ROY KELLEY, ARCHITECT

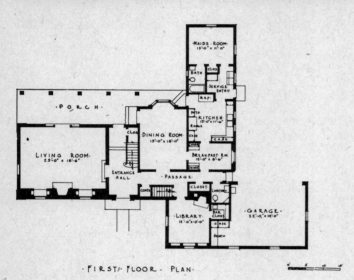

·FIRST·FLOOR·PLAN·

·SECOND·FLOOR·PLAN·

## DESCRIPTIVE OUTLINE

### EXTERIOR

| | |
|---|---|
| WALLS | Special size adobe brick veneer and cement plaster |
| ROOF | Wood shingles |
| WINDOWS | Steel casement |
| COLOR | Walls—soft pastel green Roof—natural Trim, blinds and doors —white |

### INTERIOR

| | |
|---|---|
| FLOORS | Living rooms, bedrooms and halls—oak Kitchen—linoleum Baths—tile |
| WALLS | Library—pine, stained honey color and waxed Elsewhere—plaster |
| CEILINGS | Plaster, painted |

This comfortable plan satisfies all the demands made upon a house. There is a complete assortment of rooms, and such extras as a bar closet off the library, a closet under the stairs for porch furnishings, and a generous linen closet with a window.

The large house may well include an upstairs sitting room for every-day use, leaving the living room for more formal occasions, and the library for work and study. Then again, this room may be connected with a bedroom and bath to form a pleasant suite for someone who lives with the family, but does not take part in all their activities, and wishes a certain privacy. However, to rely upon a sitting room as the only passage to a bedroom, as done here, precludes ever using the former as another bedroom.

The master bedroom suite here is a happy solution to the problem of efficiently utilizing the second-floor area over the living room when it is separated from the rest of the house by a stair hall. The small hall makes bedroom, dressing room and bath equally convenient, and obviates the necessity of passing through one to reach another.

GARDNER A. DAILEY, ARCHITECT

SECOND FLOOR PLAN

FIRST FLOOR PLAN

## DESCRIPTIVE OUTLINE

### EXTERIOR

| | |
|---|---|
| WALLS | Brick veneer and red-Wood casement |
| ROOF | Slate |
| WINDOWS | Wood casement |
| COLOR | Walls, trim and blinds —white<br>Roof—black<br>Doors—grey |

### INTERIOR

| | |
|---|---|
| FLOORS | Living rooms, bed-rooms and halls—oak<br>Baths—cork and lino-leum |
| WALLS | Plaster |
| CEILINGS | Living room and hall—Douglas spruce V-jointed<br>Elsewhere—plaster |
| LIGHTING | Flush ceiling boxes and indirect reflectors |
| CUBAGE | 64,717 cubic feet ex-clusive of garage |

The controlling factor in the design of this house was obviously the steep hillside location. The long, restful lines of the gently-pitched roofs with the deep overhang, the stubby chimneys and the unpretentious banks of large casement windows contribute a feeling of repose. This is a quality particularly to be desired in a building on a slope so that it will appear to rest firmly on the ground.

The motor court is below the street level. The entry, a few steps lower, is between floors. However, there is no feeling of coming on to a cramped stair landing, as is sometimes the case with this arrangement, for the first and second floor halls open out as one. The two-story window unfolds immediately the glorious view beyond. The whole attenuated plan from the brick wall of the loggia that screens the garage to the low service wing at the other end fits the topography without wasteful cutting and filling of earth.

Stair hall shown on page 66.

# Index to
# EXTERIORS

# Index to
# INTERIORS